Practical Information Architecture

A hands-on approach to structuring successful websites

Almost everyone who uses a pencil will use a computer, and although most people will not do any serious programming, almost everyone will be a potential customer for serious programs of some kind. Furthermore, such a mass market will require mass distribution. Analogues of bookstores, newsstands and magazine subscriptions seem plausible, as well as the kind of mail-order and home improvement marketing patterns we have now.

Butler W. Lampson
Xerox PARC, 1972

Practical Information Architecture

A hands-on approach to structuring successful websites

Eric L. Reiss

Addison Wesley

An Imprint of Pearson Education

*Harlow, England London New York Reading, Massachusetts San Francisco
Toronto Don Mills, Ontario Sydney Tokyo Singapore Hong Kong Seoul Taipei
Cape Town Madrid Mexico City Amsterdam Munich Paris Milan*

PEARSON EDUCATION LIMITED

Head Office:
Edinburgh Gate
Harlow CM20 2JE
England
Tel: +44 (0)1279 623623
Fax: +44 (0)1279 431059

London Office:
128 Long Acre
London WC2E 9AN
Tel: +44 (0)207 477 2000
Fax: +44 (0)207 240 5771
Website: www.aw.com/cseng

First published in Great Britain in 2000
© Pearson Education Limited 2000

The right of Eric L. Reiss to be identified as the author of this Work has been asserted by him in accordance with the Copyright, Designs and Patents Acts 1988.

ISBN 0-201-72590-8

British Library Cataloguing-in Publication Data
A CIP catalogue record for this book can be obtained from the British Library.

Library of Congress Cataloging in Publication Data
Applied for.

The programs in this book have been included for their instructional value. The Publisher does not offer any warranties or representations in respect of their fitness for a particular purpose, nor does the Publisher accept any liability for any loss or damage arising from their use.

Many of the designations used by manufacturers and sellers to distinguish their products are claimed as trademarks. Pearson Education Limited has made every attempt to supply trademark information about manufacturers and their products mentioned in this book. A list of trademark designations and their owners appear on p. vi.

10 9 8 7 6 5 4 3 2 1

Typeset by Mathematical Composition Setters Ltd, Salisbury, Wiltshire.
Printed and bound in the USA.

The Publishers' policy is to use paper manufactured from sustainable forests.

To Dorthe,
with all my love

TRADEMARK NOTICE

PERMISSIONS ACKNOWLEDGMENT

About this book

This is a book for people who want to create better websites. It will show you how to create an underlying *structure* so your site communicates your ideas, promotes your services, and sells your goods. In many ways, this structure is like an architectural blueprint – but instead of showing the builders where to put the *kitchen*, the structure maps out the location of the *information* you want to share with those who visit your site. The structure is the "blueprint" of the information architect.

A well-designed structure helps the designer create more effective graphics and navigation. It helps the programmer write the code. And most important of all, it keeps your visitors from getting lost, frustrated, or bored.

Unfortunately, most people don't think about the structure; in fact most people don't even know such a thing exists. Instead, they plunge ahead with the more entertaining parts of a web project, like the graphics and typefaces, and let the structure grow naturally – like weeds in a garden.

It doesn't have to be that way ...

Acknowledgements

There may only be one author's name on the cover, but an incredible number of people have generously contributed their unique skills and insights throughout this project. I have been truly fortunate to have such a supportive network and hope I haven't left anyone out!

First of all, I'd like to thank Claus Bruun, Ole Brink-Olsen, Guus Osterbaan, Bill Riley, and Ali Shah for suffering through my unpolished early drafts. I'd also like to thank Alison J. Head for her candid comments on one of the later versions, and Tim Ostler from iXL London, who inspired key additions to what eventually became the final manuscript.

My sincere thanks also go out to Karsten Pers for teaching me the nuts and bolts of search engines, to Lotte Hummer for letting me showcase the Toftejorg project, and to Arne Lycke for letting me pick apart the Nilfisk-Advance site.

During the course of gathering illustrations, I've had the pleasure of corresponding with site representatives and webmasters around the world. Although the individual companies are thanked elsewhere, I'd like to mention a few of these folks specifically for their help and support: Mia Ahmann, Maria Banchik, Marianne Bentsen, Mick Brin, Scott Beveridge, José Cavazos, Lars Peter Christensen, Robin Christensen, Jürgen deGraeve, Anders Edholm, Vanda Harris, Stefanie Kaehler, Gini Keating, Jesper Madsen, Tom Redder, Mats Renée, Michael Saxtorph, Jim Shamlin, Kathleen Vrijmoet, and Jim Wilson.

I must single out three individuals who have gone far beyond the calls of duty and friendship during the writing of this book. For starters, I owe a big hug (and a good dinner) to Rita Lenstrup of the Copenhagen Business School, who was an early champion of the book and played a major role in bringing it to print. Also, Søren Pedersen, usability expert par excellence, read and reread countless drafts and made numerous valuable suggestions. My debt to him is enormous. And last (but certainly not least), my most heartfelt thanks to Lotte Birger, my own personal web guru, who was the very first to read and comment on the manuscript. More recently, Lotte spent several long evenings helping me with the screen captures, designing special screens, and constructing structural diagrams. Lotte, thanks for putting up with me these many years and teaching me so much along the way!

The folks at Pearson Education have also been simply fantastic. Trine Barenkopf brought the manuscript to the attention of my patient and understanding editor, Michael Strang. Katherin Ekstrom, Susan Harrison, and Marilyn StClair deftly guided the manuscript through the production phase, ably assisted by designers Mike Rogers and Melinda Welch. I thank you all for turning *my* words into *our* book.

Many others have made valuable contributions of a more practical nature – knowingly or not – so let me take this opportunity to express my gratitude to Irene Constantin, Bob Cowden, Fintan Damgaard, Ebbe Høst, Søren Kerrn, Jesper Bove-Nielsen, George A. Fathauer, Frank Hansen, Bent Høier, Butler Lampson, Søren Muus, Lars Fløe Nielsen, Ivana Novosel, Per Olesen, Rico Priesner, Jannie Rasmussen, Janet Sturis, Michael Svinth, Jesper Traun, Anthony Wellman, Christina Wodtke, and the staff of Cross-Border Communications. Hats off to all of you!

And finally, when it comes to moral support, I'd like to thank my longtime mentor, Mogens Sørensen, who pestered me at regular intervals to write another book (although this isn't the book he had in mind), my mother, Louise Reiss, who introduced me to data sorting with notched cards and knitting needles when my playmates were still pondering the wonders of Silly Putty, and my wonderful wife, Dorthe, who (among many other sacrifices) took me off KP for the duration. I love you all!

Eric Reiss
Copenhagen, September 2000

Main menu

Part II Mechanics

Setting the scene

All of us have discovered websites we think are terrific because they're practical, entertaining, informative, helpful, efficient, friendly, visually pleasing, or have some other quality we appreciate. Then there all those awful sites we surf through once and hope we'll never need to visit again. But what is a bad website? For *me*, it's one that makes it hard to find the information I need or difficult to carry out the transaction I want to make.

For every outstanding website, there are probably a thousand bad ones; and not just sites put together by enthusiastic amateurs, frequently those of large international corporations are just as poor. Of all these sites, about half fail because of badly designed graphics – forcing visitors to sit through interminable downloads, read illegible typefaces, or cope with distracting visual gimmicks. Many of the remaining 50 percent also suffer from poor visual design, but their basic problem is far greater: visitors leave in frustration because the designers simply didn't organize the content in a very convenient way.

These sites hide useful information under improbable menu headings or, worse still, forget to include important details (sizes, prices, even basic contact information). They waste their visitors' time. They waste their company's money. They damage their company's image. They don't get repeat traffic. They don't communicate their ideas effectively. Most important of all, they fail to promote their goods and services.

Granted, judging the quality of a website is highly subjective, but who really cares whether 50 percent of them feature poor organization or 48.6 percent or 34.8 percent; no matter how you cut it, the problem is enormous. In fact, the 30 January 2000 issue of the weekly news magazine, *Time*, had some interesting statistics: during the period July '98 to July '99, 3.2 million people opened online bank accounts in the United States – a very impressive result. However, during that same period, 3.1 million Americans *closed* their e-bank accounts. Half of those who gave up explained that they were unhappy with the customer service or thought *the sites were too complicated!* Good information architecture is one of the keys to avoiding this kind of business disaster.

1.1 Defining information architecture

At a conference in Boston in April 2000, arranged by the American Society for Information Science, 400 bright and talented individuals spent an entire weekend trying to do just this: define information architecture. The conference was an enormous success in terms of professional networking, but it failed to agree on a definition.

Part of the problem was that individual "information architects" often perform radically different tasks depending on their specific job and educational experience. For example, experts with a background in library science frequently deal with issues that benefit from their extensive knowledge of indexing and cataloging techniques. On the other hand, someone with a computer science background is more likely to focus on the design and integration of databases. Nevertheless, both are information architects (and yes, I realize that I have generalized with regard to their respective talents).

I'm not sure that any single, all-encompassing definition will ever be found – nor am I convinced that it's necessary to do so ("engineers" gave up years ago). However, for the purposes of *this* book, "information architecture" deals with the arrangement of browser-based information (more specifically, the internal relationships between individual web pages) so visitors can do whatever they came to do with as little effort (and confusion) as possible.

Unfortunately, the importance of information architecture as it relates to the web is vastly underrated, frequently misunderstood, and usually ignored, as demonstrated by the millions of amateurish sites lurking about cyberspace. It's interesting to note that while hundreds of books have been written on web design, only a handful deal with information architecture. Nevertheless, if you're game, the following pages have been put together so your site can succeed where so many others have failed!

We all learned the basics long ago

Remember when you had to write term papers in school? The chances are, you began by sketching an outline – starting with an introduction and ending with a conclusion. In between, you organized your information in logical sections that helped you build your story and gather your thoughts. This is what information architecture is all about: arranging information in a logical fashion.

Naturally, a term paper is something that is meant to be read in a linear fashion, which is equally true of most other articles and virtually all fiction. On the other hand, encyclopedias, magazines, user manuals, and other multi-author/multi-subject works are designed to let you jump to a specific entry or article rather than forcing you to read the whole publication from end to end. A website is similar, with the added advantage of hypertext, which lets you flip to a new page, chapter, or volume with a single click.

Encyclopedias arrange subjects in alphabetical order. Reference books have a list of chapters and often an index. Magazines usually feature a contents list. We all understand these conventions and normally don't give them much thought. A website *ought* to provide some similar set of guidelines, but since the web is a relatively new medium, everybody has been busy inventing their own wheel and only a few universal conventions have been established.

Good information architecture is the key to making sure that people get the best possible value from their visit to your site. However, this involves much more than just defining half a dozen menu items on your opening page. It's also a question of defining and arranging the information that's found *under* each of these main headings in a sensible manner. It's about determining the proper level of detail each time a visitor gets deeper into the site. Information architecture is about setting basic goals for the site and identifying any other information that must be included if the site is to achieve these goals. It's about establishing one-to-one relationships with visitors. But I'm getting ahead of myself ...

1.2 Who needs to know?

Quite frankly, anyone who is involved in website production ought to become familiar with the principles described in this book. For the most part, websites are designed by teams of specialists: writers, graphic designers, programmers, webmasters, and consultants to name but a few. For large complex sites, for large complex organizations, the team members often include representatives from a management consulting company (strategic issues), an advertising agency or web house (concept, communication, usability), a system integrator (technical issues) and, of course, the client company.

If you're building a site for yourself, you may wear all of these hats simultaneously. If you come from a large company, you may wear only one. If you come from an advertising agency or production house, you probably share some of these duties with your clients. But whatever your role, your understanding of the basics of information architecture will have a direct impact on the success of your site.

So who is the information architect?

In practice, the answer to this question varies. Assuming the future site owner doesn't leave the job to their neighbor's kid, companies will sometimes call in an information architecture specialist, either as an independent consultant or from one of the professional organizations mentioned earlier. If no one on the web team understands the importance of the architecture, which often seems to be the case, the site structure may well be based on some quick whiteboard scribblings (as shown in Figure 1.1) that have been passed on to some hapless programmer – the neighbor's kid, for example.

Figure 1.1

Quick whiteboard or flipover sketches are all too frequently passed on to a programmer in the optimistic hope that these scribblings will provide the foundation for a good website. They rarely do!

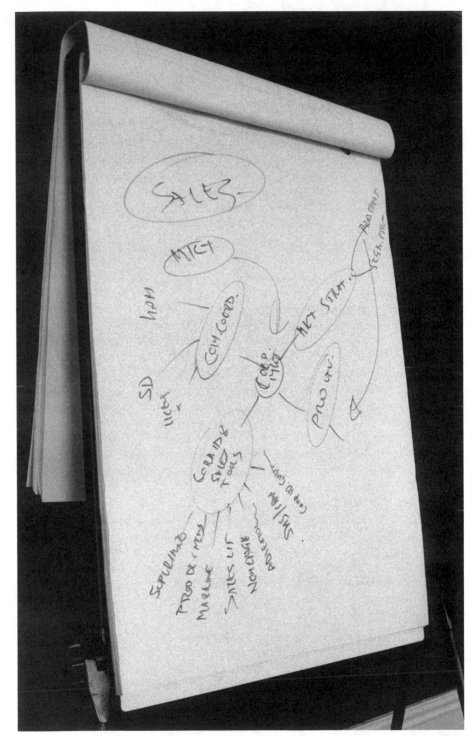

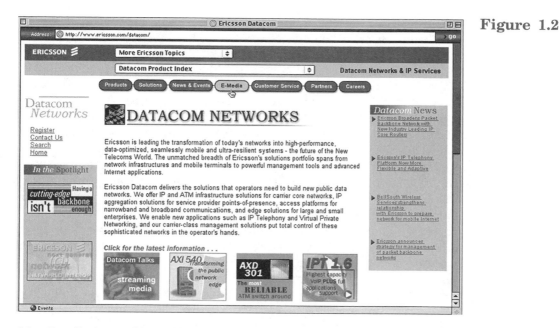

Figure 1.2

It's virtually impossible to divorce the issues of site architecture, usability, and design. They must all work together in close harmony if a site is to provide real value.

More and more, though, the role of the information architect falls to one of the key content providers, often a writer. This is usually a pretty good choice since arrangement of the written information frequently determines important navigation and design issues, for example, the use of hyperlinks embedded within the main content of a page. It helps when the person who is working on the basic structure has a reasonable idea as to how he or she will tackle the actual writing later on. Bear in mind that professional writers and journalists (particularly those who specialize in public relations and business-to-business marketing) are traditionally people who are skilled in organizing similar information for other media: brochures, annual reports, press releases, articles, etc. That said, a website is a new beast entirely, and significantly more complicated than a standard sales brochure since it is *not* linear. Moreover, it's almost impossible to divorce the strictly structural issues from those of design and navigation as these must work in close harmony if the site is to provide real value to its users – tasks that call for skills you don't learn at a school of journalism or in a creative writing class.

1.3 What skills are needed?

Success in this field seems more closely related to *how* one thinks rather than *what* one thinks. As such, your specific academic background is less important than you might imagine. However, the key criteria for success are virtually always the same: a good understanding of the site's goals and the subject matter to be presented, and a firm grasp of basic navigational techniques and related design issues – which is why this book often contains information about tasks that are not necessarily the direct responsibility of the information architect. Moreover, successful information architects must be able to reason logically, practice common sense, and relate well to others on the web team. Good communications skills (verbal and written) are essential.

As yet, there are relatively few places a budding information architect can receive a formalized education, although increasing numbers of university-level "schools of library science" are becoming "schools of information" in order to meet the growing need for trained specialists. Currently, many professional information architects have degrees in either computer or library science, but even so, a surprising number of first-rate architects have trained in completely unrelated disciplines.

In years to come, I suspect business schools will make information architecture part of their curriculum, since the web is very much a market communications tool. For this reason, the first few chapters of this book contain some basic business information that you may find valuable. If you went to business school, please forgive me for any oversimplification of these important issues.

1.4 Size doesn't matter (much)

It may come as a surprise, but the size of the site you're planning is of relatively little consequence. That's because the basic problems of information architecture are *generic* and therefore apply equally to a Fortune 500 company and a site designed to sell your friend's handmade candles. Yes, there's much more work to be done with a site consisting of 30,000 pages in relation to one with only a dozen or so, but it's like painting a wall – the basic technique is the same no matter whether you're swinging a brush at your garage door or the Great Wall of China. In other words, although this book was written for people involved in the creation of fairly comprehensive business websites, a site doesn't have to have more than a few pages before you can start putting these techniques to good use.

1.5 You have both a product and a customer

Not all of what you'll find described in this book will necessarily have relevance for your particular site. For example, if you're selling handmade candles, you probably won't be terribly interested in a discussion of subsidiaries and distributors. My advice? Read the subheads and jump ahead

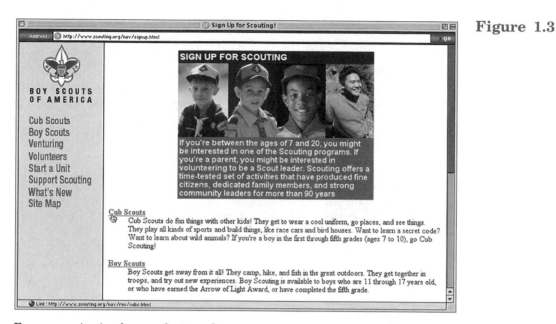

Every organization has products and customers, even non-commercial enterprises.

to the next section that deals with something you *are* interested in. One assumption I *have* made is that you have both a *product* and a *customer*. But don't take these labels too literally or assume that money is changing hands. For example, if you're building a site for the local Boy Scouts, your "product" may be an idea (character, citizenship, personal fitness) and your "customers" may be teenage boys (Figure 1.3). Remember, too, *information* itself is a valuable commodity and can also, therefore, be considered a "product."

1.6 About common sense

I rather expect you to say "How dumb does this guy think I am?" at regular intervals. After all, this is how people usually react to common-sense explanations: and above all else, successful information architecture hinges on common sense. However, common sense doesn't work unless you've actually identified a problem and given it some thought. Here's an example.

Have you ever wondered why the direction signals on your car's steering column are located where they are? When turn signals were first adopted back in the 1920s, someone had to make a decision as to where to put them since there were no precedents to draw on. The solution was not based on personal preference or aesthetics, it's pure common sense.

Here's a hint: in countries where people drive on the right, like the US, the signals are placed on the left-hand side of the steering column. For many years, however, the UK, Japan, and other countries where they drive on the left, had signals located on the right.*

And here's the answer. Usually, when you are about to make a turn, you need to slow the car at roughly the same time you need to signal. If you have to shift gears manually, it makes sense to put the signals on the opposite side of the steering column from the gear shift so that one hand is always on the wheel. At this point, you're probably saying, "And so what?" The point is, did you ever think about this before? Probably not, because someone has already done the thinking for you.

A good information architect thinks about the problems of arranging information on the site so that visitors aren't forced to guess-and-click their way from page to page. The decisions you make now are critical since they directly affect your visitors' behavior and ultimately their opinion of your site.

1.7 Structuring a website can't be learned in a linear fashion

Ideally, this would be one of those how-to books that promises you a "five-step plan for success" or something along those lines. Unfortunately, that's not the way things work in real life and sometimes you'll have to take several different things into account simultaneously. Although I've tried to present the process as a logical chain of events, I've occasionally added a few comments about some subject discussed later in the book to help you make a decision at an earlier stage. Don't be afraid to skip around as you read, but don't forget to look at the parts you missed either. Learning to understand information architecture is like completing one of those connect-the-dot puzzles: you can't see the big picture until you've worked through the whole thing.

1.8 Heard all this before? (a note to experienced information architects)

Those of you who have extensive experience in website production will probably be disappointed to find that this book talks about subjects and techniques with which you are already familiar. However, remember, you are members of a select minority in this relatively new field – some may say "pioneers." Please forgive me if I dwell on things that you consider

---

* Today, virtually all turn signals are located on the left due to the increased popularity of automatic transmission and the need to design economical, universal parts that can be used in both home and export markets.

second-nature, or only devote a paragraph or two to a subject that you have made your life's work. My purpose here is not to chart new territory but to help explain some of the territory that has already been charted – to lay a foundation that will help today's readers become the pioneers of tomorrow. I feel this is tremendously important if our field is to develop and mature.

1.9 Defining a few terms

Since the same word often means different things to different people, here are *my* definitions of some of the words that may cause confusion. Not all of them are necessarily used in this book, but you'll invariably encounter them in discussions with other website developers so here they are.

By the way, as you'll probably read this list in a linear fashion, related terms have been grouped together, and frequently, an individual definition will be directly linked to that of the previous word. Hence, alphabetical order, as an underlying structure, seemed to be a silly convention. However, for future reference, an alphabetical list appears in the glossary.

web refers to the World Wide Web (WWW), which, for our purposes here, is more or less synonymous with the internet, although technically speaking the internet is a physical structure and the web is what the internet became with the introduction of HTML.

HTML (HyperText Markup Language) the programming language used to create websites, the brainchild of WWW founder Tim Berners-Lee.

URL (Uniform Resource Locator) the means by which an exact location on the internet is identified, another Berners-Lee development. The URL appears in the address line in the browser window, for example, http://www.anycompany.com.

website represents the complete interrelated collection of pages and links that are created and maintained by a single owner.

site synonymous for website

site owner the person or organization with overall responsibility for the design and editorial content of the site. For example, AltaVista would be the site owner for the search engine Altavista.com.

subsite an autonomous site, often with a narrow target audience, that is a spin-off from another site, generally with a broader audience. Sometimes for purposes of differentiation, the more general site is called the main site, although occasionally, two related sites may regard each other as subsites. CNN.com and the subsite for Sports Illustrated magazine, CNNSI.com, are a good case in point.

page all the information that appears on the screen following a single mouse-click.

subpage a page (generally more detailed) related directly to some preceding page.

structure the detailed diagram or text outline that indicates the subject content of every page in a website and how it relates to the other pages on the site or links to external pages. Many professional information architects call these "Visiograms," named after the PC program used to create them.

architecture often this term is synonymous with structure, although structure usually refers to a specific project-related diagram whereas architecture relates more to the overall generic concept of informational organization.

visitor a person who enters a website. Sometimes called a *user*, although I generally prefer *visitor* since this implies that the person in question is an outsider rather than someone directly connected with the site owner's organization. On the other hand, since a website is really an *application*, visitors are, in fact, users and I therefore use both terms.

homepage generally, the first page that greets a visitor when visiting a particular website. Some people still insist on referring to the entire site as a homepage, which is a hangover from the old days when a site rarely *had* more than one page. If you're still calling websites homepages, it's time you got out of the habit!

menu a list of choices. In web terms, these choices usually function as individual links to other pages.

main menu often used as a synonym for homepage, but in the strictest terms refers specifically to the top-level (primary) navigational choices. I use the phrase in both ways.

taxonomy the study of the general principles of scientific classification. Often, information architects use the term to represent a particular hierarchical structure. For example, the underlying structures of two distinct main-menu choices may be referred to as "parallel taxonomies."

splash screen one or more pages that have been designed to welcome a visitor to the main page of a website (Figure 1.4). A large corporate logo with a hyperlink stating "Click here to enter site" is a typical example. Also called an "entry tunnel." Navigational options are usually quite limited, but sometimes these screens are used by international organizations to give visitors a choice of languages before they enter the site proper.

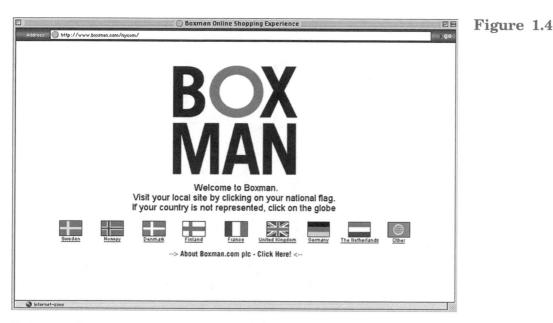

Figure 1.4

Boxman is Europe's leading online source for music CDs. Their "splash" screen channels visitors directly to local content in a range of national languages.

link any text or graphic device that brings visitors to a new page when clicked.

hyperlink for the purposes of this book, a hyperlink is a link that forms part of the editorial content of the page rather than a graphic button in the primary navigation. In most instances, hyperlinks are set in the ordinary text font, underlined, and in a contrasting color. However, small graphics can also function as hyperlinks if they are located within the content area of the page.

primary navigation the general menu choices that are repeated on most (if not all) of the pages contained in the site. Sometimes called the main menu.

local navigation navigational choices leading to subtopics defined by one of the main-menu subjects as shown in Figure 1.5.

site tools sometimes called global navigation or functional navigation, devices in this category refer to search engines, site maps, etc. that let you immediately jump from one page on the site to another without drilling down through a hierarchy. Site tools, however, can also include the contact page and other subjects of a more general, practical nature.

contextual navigation the collection of related links on a page that allows visitors to immediately click to subject-related pages, even

Figure 1.5

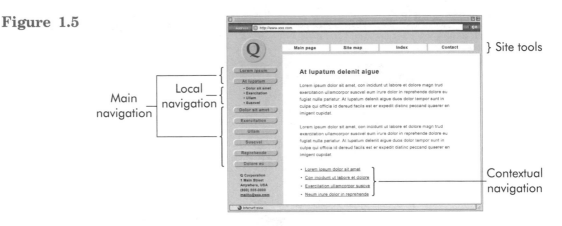

This sample screen shows some typical navigational options.

when these pages actually "live" under another menu heading. In traditional library terms, this is known as "cross-referencing."

pop-up a small screen or graphic "bubble" that is superimposed on a screen when you click a particular area. For example, many Windows programs use pop-up "help" bubbles.

rollover a dynamic device that changes the appearance of the page when the cursor moves over a particular area without the user having to click. Buttons that change color when the cursor is correctly positioned are rollovers. However, sometimes rollovers can contain explanatory text, particularly in conjunction with a diagram or photograph.

drop-down a menu that expands when it is clicked, for example, those menus located at the top of the screen in virtually all Windows and Macintosh applications.

content this word has two distinct uses in this book. In most instances, content refers merely to the *subject* discussed on a particular page. However, in rare instances it may also refer to editorial content.

editorial content refers to *specific information*, including all the words, photographs, graphics, and other page-specific elements that appear on a site. Sometimes I've shortened editorial content to "content" for the sake of readability if the proper context seemed obvious.

content provider someone who supplies editorial content, usually written, although photographs and graphics are also content elements.

syndicated content dynamic editorial content created by a third party and made available for wider distribution via subscription. For example, stock prices on a banking site are a classic example of syndicated content.

content management the process of transferring editorial content (text and graphics) to a website in a controlled and organized manner and/or editing existing browser-based content.

granularity the extent to which a larger piece of information has been broken down into smaller units. For example, this book is broken down into individual chapters, each of which features its own set of sections. The content of an individual subhead is the smallest "grain" in this particular work. On a website, the more subdivisions you create in a document, the greater the granularity and thus the greater the dynamics of the site. There are limitations, though – after all, sometimes a cracker is better than a handful of crumbs.

surface often used as a verb as in "to surface information," which means to bring information to a higher level within the overall hierarchy or to create contextual links that make it easier for visitors to find related information located elsewhere on the site.

customization what a visitor does to a site when setting personal preferences (turning off graphics, arranging content, etc.)

personalization what a site does to *itself* in terms of altering navigation according to the perceived needs of an individual visitor. By and large, personalization is used to provide improved contextual navigation.

e-commerce the specific process of selling goods or services from a website.

e-business a broad, catch-all term for the transactions and other business operations that use the web as the basic communications infrastructure. In other words, a company can practice e-business by using their site for lead generation without actually conducting e-commerce.

layout the physical positioning of graphic and text elements on a web page.

wireframes the skeletal design templates for generic pages, indicating the correct position of individual elements including text, graphics, navigation, banner ads, etc.

design within the context of this book, design almost always refers to the visual appearance of a web page. Design elements include all graphics, such as buttons, logos, animations, photographs, etc., plus background colors and text fonts. That said, I sometimes use the phrase "designing a site" in the broader sense to reflect both structural *and* graphical considerations.

HCI (Human–Computer Interaction) the study of how people relate to electronic tools and interfaces. Also called CHI.

GUI (Graphical User Interface) the revolutionary "desktop-cursor-icon" concept (including menus, folders, and files) developed by Xerox PARC in the 1970s, first exploited commercially by Apple in 1983 with the launch of the Macintosh. Xerox PARC's use of the computer mouse for point-and-click operations was also an integral part of this concept.

UML (Unified Modeling Language) an object-oriented analysis/design method for visualizing, specifying, constructing, and documenting informational relationships – a hot information architecture topic these days.

usability for the purposes of this book, usability deals with how visitors perceive the *functionality* of a particular website. The ergonomic aspects of usability (for example, whether visitors can actually *find* a particular link on a screen) are not discussed in any detail.

WAP (Wireless Application Protocol) an open communication standard that allows people to access dynamic content from mobile devices, primarily telephones.

Defining the task

The first time the "Web Task Force" (or whatever your group calls itself) gets together, everybody is enthusiastic and everybody has an opinion that they are eager to share with the rest of the group. This enthusiasm, though, rapidly gives way to boredom and frustration as talk turns from the more exciting aspects of the project (flaming logos and other eyecatching features) to down-to-earth realities, the most important of which is defining the goals of the website. Nevertheless, this is the place to start, especially if you're the information architect.

2.1 A brief introduction to the site development process

In order to put information architecture in its proper working perspective, let's first take a look at the basic steps that form the *process* of creating or improving a website. I've divided this into seven steps, but there are many models that follow the same basic structure (with more or fewer divisions depending on the level of detail). My Seven A's are as follows:

1 **Allocate** the financial and human resources needed to tackle the project, including those for any promotional activities designed to generate site traffic.

2 **Analyze** the project in terms of strategic goals, target audiences, and methods for measuring the success of the site. If an existing site needs to be improved, this phase will also involve usability testing of the current version.

3 **Architect** the site and define the site's functional concept: to develop a diagram showing the proper relationship between all the individual pages. Although the information architect is involved to varying degrees in *all* of these steps, this is where he or she is most active. In large web houses, the information architect will often work alongside a usability expert, a navigation designer, and perhaps other specialists during this phase.

4 **Apply** the knowledge gained during the previous phases to the creation of design templates, graphics, and the user interface. I use

apply as in "applied arts" rather than the more common "design" since a lot more goes on at this point than just making things pretty.

5 **Accumulate** the needed content, build the databases, and write any additional software required by the informational structure. Planning the integration of existing databases or Customer Relationship Management (CRM) tools with the browser-based solution also takes place at this time.

6 **Assemble** the pages and test the site, from both a technical and a usability standpoint.

7 **Adjust** the site as new needs are defined.

The important thing to understand is that information architecture is an ongoing task, even though this book focuses on its role in the second and third phases. Moreover, the process described above is *linear* in that any attempt to short-circuit individual steps will invariably lead to problems later on. However, the process is also *circular* in that adjustment always leads back to the allocation/analysis steps as the site evolves.

If you're interested, other good process descriptions can be found at www.razorfish.com and www.agency.com. Jessica Burdman's book, *Collaborative Web Development* (Reading, MA: Addison-Wesley, 1999), is something of a "must-have" if you really mean business.

2.2 Setting your goals

With very few exceptions, there's always a reason *why* someone decided the time was right to launch (or improve) a website, quite apart from the fact that visitors have come to expect regular updates and redesigns of existing sites. Here are some of the most common goals:

- establish a new direct sales channel

- streamline existing sales routines

- reduce the need for live sales and service representatives

- reduce the need for pre-printed technical documentation

- create a web presence for lead generation

- build better customer/investor/press relationships

Let's take a closer look at each of these possible goals. They may give you a few ideas as to how to improve your own site.

New direct sales channel

Virtually any product that can be sold by mail-order catalog can also be sold online. I'll get into some of the details of e-commerce later, in particular in Chapter 6; right now, we're strictly interested in defining goals. Software products, for example, and other types of digitalized information are particularly well-suited to online sales because there are considerably fewer logistical issues to contend with in relation to physical products. In most cases, the customer simply downloads the file and pays via credit card. Since it's expensive to send out a sales rep to potential customers, many companies now offer significant discounts to customers who use their websites instead of calling the office, and have actually increased their overall profit margins despite the discounts! For example, Dell Computers claims up to 30 percent higher profit margins for products sold online.

Streamline existing sales routine

Sometimes, online sales threaten to disrupt otherwise good relationships with local distributors, which is particularly dangerous if these people also make service and maintenance calls, deal with local authorities, or perform other functions that require hands-on presence. Nevertheless, your site *can* assist local distributors by providing customers with a wide range of valuable sales information from basic product descriptions to detailed technical data sheets.

As opposed to printed brochures, the web makes it possible to distribute effective 3-D graphics and animations which serve to demonstrate functions that cannot be viewed even with the real product sitting right in front of you (Figure 2.1). If you're out to sell handmade candles, there's little need for this kind of graphic sophistication. However, if you need to show how the filtration system in a vacuum cleaner works, or the best way to load a container ship, the web can be an invaluable tool. As a rule, potential customers who have already investigated a product online ask more relevant questions in a sales situation, and are more likely to buy the product.

Reduce the need for live sales and service reps

If your customers call all day long, asking the same types of questions, a website can help reduce the load on your staff by providing online answers to frequently asked questions (FAQs in the web-bizz). Since people are no longer tied up on the phone, their talents can often be put to better use generating new leads and cementing long-term relationships with key customers. Moreover, if good basic information is available through the website, the number of individual sales calls needed to close a sale may be

Figure 2.1

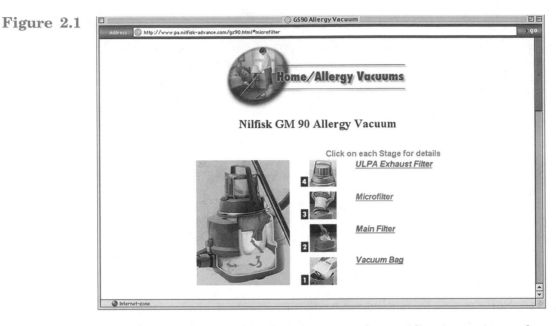

Websites can help streamline the sales process by providing interactive product demonstrations. In this example, rollover menu choices animate the cut-away graphic to illustrate each of the four filtering principles. Clicking these links provides more detailed textual information.

reduced as the initial meetings will often be far more productive. It may even be possible to reallocate resources internally or, ultimately, reduce the size of your workforce. The current buzzword for this is "disintermediation," which means to cut out the middleman.

Reduce the need for pre-printed documentation

Did you know that the owner's manual for a new Mazda is 37 times as long as the US Constitution? And, hand on heart, did you really read all of the enormous guide that came with your copy of Windows '95? No wonder more and more product documentation is published electronically. It costs a lot of money to print and distribute technical information and most people don't want it anyway. If your company has to distribute a lot of paper, why not put these documents on your website instead? And if your documentation is updated regularly, there's even more reason to put it on the web (as opposed to a CD-ROM) since it provides a convenient central location for update activities and guarantees site visitors access to the very latest information.

On the other hand, your visitors don't necessarily want to download huge documents, which means you'll probably want to restructure your documentation for the web. After all, the need for documentation occurs when people need a specific *answer* to a specific *question*. In other words, they don't necessarily want the answers to everybody else's questions, too.

Create web presence for lead generation

Back in 1983, fax machines were the exception rather than the rule. Two years later, virtually every company had one. The same is true of websites, and today most companies have an online presence. In fact, increasing numbers of companies *are* websites. In short, if your company doesn't have a site, it is high time they did. (If they do, I'll assume you're reading this because you suspect it could be better.)

A website gives a company a chance to establish themselves as an authority in their field. The cumulative knowledge that builds up in an organization is often enormous and the web provides a perfect forum for displaying this know-how, which is usually invisible to the rest of the world. On-site resource libraries provide an excellent opportunity to publish company-produced white papers and other background information to prove that companies have been doing their homework. Detailed and authoritative FAQ lists show that companies really know what they're talking about. And reference stories show that companies practice what they preach.

One word of warning: with the advent of the PC, it's easy to keep electronic documents on file that would have been thrown out years ago had they been on paper. Remember, just because you *have* a document, you don't necessarily want to clutter up your site with information that has little or no value to your site's visitors. This is why sites that were once well-architected so often get out of hand.

Here's a little success story. One of the companies I've worked with provides very expensive and very specialized engineering services and equipment. The company felt that since they were practically a household name in their well-defined industry, a website was merely an expensive gimmick. Nevertheless, someone in the company approved the project and the agency I was working for got the job. Within a week of their online debut, the company had landed an order for over $3 million from a previously unknown customer. Now, three years later, their site plays a key role in their job recruitment efforts, training programs, and of course, lead generation.

Build better customer/investor/press relationships

Nowadays, everyone is talking about "one-to-one" business relationships and a website is frequently the key to creating them. In essence, a one-to-one relationship implies that you treat customers differently according to their specific needs. Although most web visitors are anonymous, a lot of information can be gained simply by monitoring click patterns as visitors work their way through your site. Sites can either be automatically configured to reflect the visitors' preferences, or the site can ask questions of the visitor along the way and suggest specific areas they might like to investigate further. However, even without sophisticated customization tools, the basic site architecture can still be arranged to cater to individual needs and expectations. You can read more about some of the most common techniques in Chapter 16.

A large website is sometimes segmented so that certain portions are only visible to selected audiences via password or registration. This, too, helps bring visitors and the site's owner closer together. For example, a Press Lounge can let journalists download background information, press releases, high-resolution photos of products, people, etc. Investors can gain access to the latest financial information or other news, and customers can use the site to track transactions that have to do with them and them alone.

Rescuing the service sector

Companies that provide a service consisting solely of selling someone else's products – travel agents, for example – are in real trouble these days. With the advent of online services, it's important for these companies to use the web to their advantage rather than view it as a threat. If we pursue the travel agent path for a moment, let's pause to think about *why* these companies were initially formed. Well, first of all, it was difficult to deal directly with airlines and their hundreds of obscure pricing systems. Second, it was convenient for people to book both transportation and accommodation at the same time. Third, travel agents spent a lot of their time actually travelling, so they could provide their customers with first-hand knowledge of faraway places.

So where's the problem? Do you really want to log on to the British Airways site, followed by the Marriott site, followed by the Hertz site, followed by the site for a theater, concert hall, restaurant, and so on? Probably not. Besides, how are you going to learn about that great little hotel on the Left Bank in Paris that costs next to nothing but is clean, tidy and right in the middle of all the action? Answer: contact your travel agent.

The dilemma of the service sector is strictly imaginary. If a company has provided a useful service in the past, their job is to work out how they can transfer this kind of ease-of-use and experience to the web. Granted, the process will probably not be 100 percent browser based, but that doesn't matter (Figure 2.2). An online query from a customer or potential customer is just as good as a phone call: the site exists to encourage interaction. Moreover, a website makes it easy to track customer preferences, a service many "service" companies have ignored in the past.

Figure 2.2

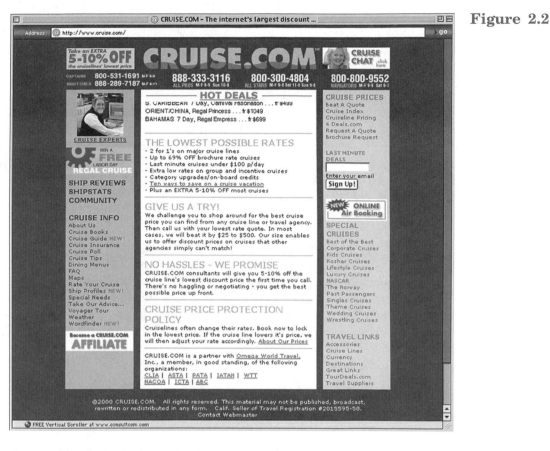

Transactions don't always need to be 100 percent browser-based. Here, prominently displayed telephone numbers and numerous links encourage visitors to contact Cruise.com directly for personalized service.

Keep your main goal in focus

Although your website may have several goals, remember that *one* goal will always be more important than the others. Goals, although not mutually exclusive, tend to get shuffled around simply because some are easier to attain than others – the people paying the bills usually want to implement the easy stuff first. Invariably, goal-driven features that require a basic change in established company attitudes and procedures, such as registering information in an electronic database rather than on paper forms, will be more difficult to implement.

Basic goals are pushed aside more frequently than you might expect. For example, I once worked with a company that needed an online product catalog. As the project got rolling, internal politics shifted the site's focus to presenting the detailed business structure and historical background for each of about 30 worldwide subsidiaries. Not very interesting for customers, but fascinating for the employees in the field. By the time all this was in place, there was no budget left for the online catalog – so this was put on the back burner where it is still waiting to boil. Now, the company is wondering why the website isn't generating the leads it should! The lesson to be learned is this: if the thrust of the site changes along the way, make sure to let the decision-makers know that the initial goals may be in jeopardy.

Again, keep in mind that we are trying to identify goals at this point, not the methods needed to reach these goals, not yet at least. However, if you've already got some ideas, for goodness sake, jot them down now before you forget them!

2.3 Defining your target audience

Assuming your team already has a primary goal in mind, and probably several secondary goals too, now's the time to think about who you're going to talk to. Here are some possible target audiences:

- existing customers
- potential customers
- investors
- potential employees
- subcontractors
- distributors

or on a personal level:

- friends
- family
- basic self-promotion
    - others with a common interest (hobbies, politics, etc.)
    - potential employers (online CV etc.)

Naturally, you can divide many of these groups into potential and existing audiences according to your specific needs. You will probably also find many other audience distinctions that are unique to your company so don't hesitate to examine these possible targets. For example, if you're promoting paint, you might want to define professional painters and homeowners as two distinct customer groups with individual informational needs.

No matter what you or your web team eventually decides, just as with goals, there will always be a *primary audience* and you must keep them in focus no matter how many other groups you'd also like to address.

Chicken or egg: goals or audience?

In practice, discussions of overall goals and the primary audience take place more or less simultaneously. In other words, if you start by discussing the audience, you soon move on to goals. If you start with goals, you invariably end up talking about the audience. For example:

"We want to target our investors."

"Why?"

"We want to make them feel closer to the company by keeping them well informed. We want them to continue to think they made a good choice when they gave us their money."

Bingo! A goal has been defined: to reassure investors and keep them well informed. Although this may not end up being the primary goal, it will be important to remember when the time comes to define the nature of the editorial content that needs to be put on the site.

Goals and audiences must be in harmony

The example mentioned earlier (of the company with 30 international subsidiaries) is a classic example of how things can go wrong when the primary goal and the primary audience do not complement each other. Here, the primary goal was to increase sales through online product presentations but the audience ended up as one that was strictly internal. Granted, this was not the original plan, but that's how things worked out. If you sense that there is disharmony in the decisions being made, now is the time to voice your objections, don't wait until the damage is done.

Don't take goals for granted

If you've been wondering why I've spent so much time discussing what may already seem obvious, keep in mind that precisely *because* goal-setting is so obvious, this process tends to get overlooked. One of the biggest mistakes is to assume that everyone agrees on why and for whom the site is being produced. Even if these goals have already been dictated by someone higher up in the organization (the CEO's family always seems to have something to say), make sure that all the alternatives receive proper consideration.

In truth, if your team can get these goals and targets sorted out during the course of a single meeting, you're off to a flying start. In most cases, this process takes several long sessions, particularly if many people are involved, each with his or her own personal agenda. I don't want to scare you, but a professional management consultancy, working for a mid-sized organization, will typically budget about 200 hours for this initial strategic phase. It's often money well spent.

Your target audience also has goals

The goals of the site owner and the goals of the target audience aren't always the same. In fact, what people *need* and what they *want* are often very different. If at all possible, go out and talk to members of the proposed target audience to get a feel for how *they* would like to use the site. See if you can visit them rather than have them drop by your office, you'll learn a lot more! For example, if the purpose of the site is to help customers order replacement parts, take a look at their paper catalogs. Which sections have been well-thumbed? What pages have been bookmarked? What bits of information are stuck to this person's bulletin board? All of this will be important to remember when the time comes to decide what information should be on the site and where it should be located.

Look, also, at the general work environment. Is the atmosphere hectic? Does the phone ring every two minutes? Does this person have to do three things at once? If so, you'll have to make sure that online transactions can be interrupted without forcing the user to start all over again when he or she returns to the screen. Peter Merholz, Creative Director at Epinions.com, has coined a great word for this, "resumability." In other words, the site is designed and architected to allow visitors to pick up where they left off. In general, don't wait too long to carry out any appropriate task-analysis activities since they will invariably affect the way in which you structure your site.

2.4 Researching the organization

At one point during (or immediately following) the goal-setting process, someone is going to have to do some research within the organization, too. If you've opted for online sales, you need to know how the current sales and distribution system works so that the online solution represents a genuine improvement in terms of transaction time and customer service. If you've decided to streamline your help-desk operations, you need to identify the specific tasks the website can be expected to perform more efficiently. In fact, it often helps to talk to the company receptionist in order to gain some impression of where the incoming calls are being transferred (Figure 2.3). Not only will this information help you build a more

Please note routing of all calls when no request
was made to be connected to a specific employee:

Administration ||||| ||||| ||||| ||||| ||
Bookkeeping ||||| |||
Sales ||||| ||||| ||||| ||||| ||||| ||||| |||
Marketing ||||| ||||| ||
Development |||||
Production ||||| ||||| ||||
Quality Assurance |||
Technical support ||||| ||||| ||||| ||||| ||
Spare parts ||||| ||||| |||

Figure 2.3

In this example, the receptionist keeps a simple statistical record of incoming calls in which the caller asked for (or needed assistance from) a particular department, but didn't request a specific employee name or extension number. The tracking takes place over the course of an entire working week. Repeating this same test some months after the site's launch provides a basic indication of how the website has affected the daily work routine.

effective site, it also provides valuable comparative data when the time comes to evaluate the results of your online efforts.

All of this organizational detective work takes time, which is why professional management consultants budget so many hours for this first phase. Although expensive, outside consultants have the advantage of seeing things as they really are, and can quickly spot many of the bad habits companies pick up over the years. "But we've always done it this way!" – the battlecry of the stagnant organization – doesn't necessarily make things right or rule out room for improvement.

If you want to learn more about these information-gathering techniques (and many other related subjects), take a look at *Contextual Design* by Hugh Beyer and Karen Holtzblatt (San Francisco, CA: Academic Press/Morgan Kauffmann, 1997). It's truly a remarkable work.

Keep in mind ...

- Any attempt to short-circuit the development process by skipping individual steps will inevitably cause problems.

- Defining the goals of the site will define the target audience. This, in turn, will define the needed content.

- Don't lose sight of your main goal as the discussions progress.

- Your goals and your target audience must be in harmony.

- Your target audience will probably have different goals from those of your company.

- Don't take goals for granted. Make sure everyone on the team agrees on what they want to accomplish.

3 Measuring your success

It seems silly to start talking about the success of a website when the process is still a long way from completion. However, since an evaluation always depends on the comparison of two distinct but related pieces of information, it's important to establish a baseline prior to the site launch from which we can calculate our success. Here's a familiar example. We've all received magazine renewal cards that proclaim "Reply now and save up to 66 percent." Sounds like a good deal, assuming this calculation is based on the newsstand price and that we *know* what the newsstand price is. But since the baseline is unknown, there's no way to determine the true value of the offer. In other words, you won't know if your site actually reduced the cost of making a sale (or whatever) unless you know what it *used* to cost.

Generally speaking, there are two key parameters that can be measured from within the company: time and money. These are numerical specifics and therefore easy to compare – although gathering the data can be tricky. Externally, there are several subjective parameters, which are usually measured by conducting interviews or sending out questionnaires. Customer satisfaction surveys typically cover these "soft" issues such as service quality, ease of doing business, etc.

3.1 Measuring time and money

The specific methods you use to gather these data will depend to a great extent on your company's organization, and the amount of effort you are willing to make. If some statistical information already exists, such as a help-desk log, you're already ahead of the game. Otherwise, there's no other course than to start tracking phone time, project time, lead-generation statistics, etc. from existing channels. Actual sales statistics are tremendously important but fortunately these are usually easy to come by.

You should also check the time spent answering e-mail since this traffic will almost always increase after you go online. If your phone time goes down, but your e-mail time increases proportionally, you may not have achieved the success you thought you had. On the other hand, this may give you a clue as to how some other process can be automated via the website.

The basic questions you need to ask (and answer) are:

- How are we spending money today?
  - phone bills
  - staff salary (also external and part-time help)
  - travel expenses
  - other general overhead
  - ???

- How are we earning money today?
  - sales via market channels (distributors, subsidiaries, etc.)
  - parts and service
  - consulting
  - ???

- How are we using our time today?
  - on the phone
  - in meetings
  - answering mail
  - travelling
  - other office work
  - ???

Often, questions relating to time can be answered subjectively and still provide a usable indication for comparative purposes. For example, asking people to assign a simple percentage to each of the time categories might be sufficient. However, it's also important to differentiate between time spent on providing a standard answer to a common question and time spent solving a very specific problem or developing a closer relationship with a valued customer. Make sure to take this into account when you ask your questions.

And when you're up and running ...

After you've been online for a reasonable period – say three to six months – it's time to repeat the statistical surveys you conducted prior to the launch. Comparing the figures will help you discover if you're living up to your original goals and where you might need to fine-tune your site.

Of course, you may also need to fine-tune your staff. After all, if you've set out to create a "virtual company" based on an existing organization, you will also have to take the time to educate your people as to how the website affects their daily work, changes the way resources are allocated, and, in time, will come to alter their overall view of the organization's structure.

Charting actual site statistics can be very helpful in determining the general popularity of the site: number of user sessions, the number of links from other sites, the number of repeat visitors, etc. This, however, only tells part of the story. One of the most useful comparisons you can make is to examine the total number of visitors and then calculate the exact percentage of these visitors that have become actual customers. This provides a clear indication of the actual *success* of the site.

The manner in which you promote the site (banner ads, print ads, e-mailings, word-of-mouth) is also important. If nobody knows you exist, your site cannot possibly do its job. This should go without saying, but in practice an amazing number of site owners forget even basic marketing efforts, such as registration with the leading search engines.

Site statistics (sometimes called "webmetrics") will also tell you if you've hit your target audience. If you've aimed to please your investors, but despite a generally good number of visitors overall, no one is clicking into your investor information, one of three things may

Figure 3.1

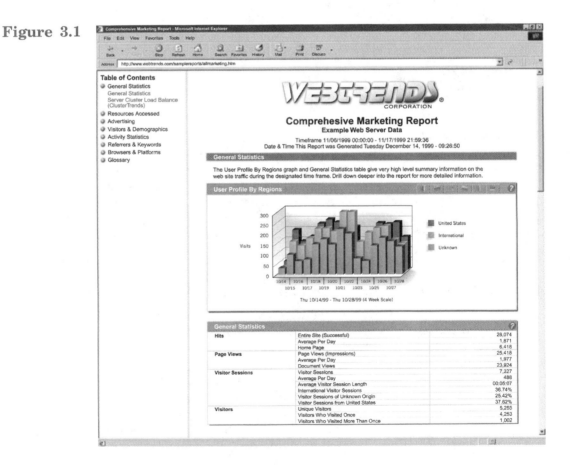

A typical WebTrends report. The table of contents on the left provides a convenient overview of the data contained in these valuable documents.

have happened:

- your target audience *doesn't know* about this information;
- your target audience *doesn't need* or *isn't interested* in this information;
- your target audience *is interested in something else* on your site.

If this occurs, it's time to consider making a few architectural and design adjustments, or advertising your site more effectively. You should probably talk to your target audience(s), too, since you may not be fulfilling *their* goals. After all, even if your site is receiving a lot of traffic, people may actually be searching in vain for information that is *not* available – but more about that in the next chapter!

For those of you who are unfamiliar with website statistics, it's important to know the difference between the number of "hits" and the number of "user sessions." Hits represent the total number of data files downloaded each time you click to a new web page. Since each individual graphic button, photo, text block, etc. counts as a hit, you'll probably get a false impression of the site's popularity. On the other hand, user sessions represent the number of individual *visitors* that have come to a site – a far more useful statistic. If you want to learn more, take a look at www.webtrends.com (Figure 3.1). They produce one of the best statistical tools around, and their site contains some sample reports that define these and other important terms.

3.2 Customer satisfaction surveys

Customer satisfaction surveys are just as important vis-à-vis websites as they are for your other operations. Typically, you'll be interested in hearing people's views on site functionality, usability, service quality, transaction speed, etc. Any comparisons that can be made between phone, mail, or personal transactions and online procedures are particularly valuable. After all, if it's still easier for your customers to pick up the phone than click through your site, you've probably done something wrong – or need to do something better.

If you already conduct regular customer satisfaction surveys, now's the time to add relevant web-related questions. You can also ask people who are actually online and visiting your site to let you know what they think; many companies encourage visitors to comment on trial pages set up specifically to measure their reactions to navigation, design, usability, etc. Remember, though, visitors are generally unhappy if they're forced to answer long questionnaires that unexpectedly appear in their browser window without having been specifically requested.

3.3 Cannibalization of existing sales channels

When dealing with online sales, it's also wise to investigate the extent to which the new site is cannibalizing existing sales channels. Cannibalization may be a good thing if you're out to cut down on your sales staff. It may be a very bad thing if you're cutting into distributor revenues that make local services possible. However, it may also be opening up new markets, in which case some cannibalization may be a small price to pay for large long-term gains.

More and more companies are treating their e-commerce sites as individual subsidiaries, repeating many of the staff functions present in their brick-and-mortar operations – sales manager, marketing director, etc. Although you may not choose to follow suit, it sometimes helps to at least *view* your site as a subsidiary, particularly from a sales–statistical standpoint.

Remember, your customers will always contact your organization in the manner most convenient for *them*. Back in 1900, customers wrote letters or sent a telegram. About 1910, they started to phone. Around 1983, they started to fax. In the mid-1990s, they started to e-mail. In short, if traditional distributors are bypassed because your website provides greater convenience, it simply means your older communications channels have become outmoded. You're welcome to resist these changes, but you're probably wiser to accept them if you want to remain competitive.

A word of warning: before you go out and fire your sales staff and drop your distributors, don't forget that these people often know a lot of important details that are usually not available from any other source in the company. In most cases it's far better to hold onto these valuable personal sales channels and redefine their role in the overall sales process.

Keep in mind ...

- Researching the organization helps establish a baseline from which the effectiveness of your site can be later measured.

- Install and use a good statistical tool to keep track of visitors.

- Site statistics are useful indicators but what you really want to know is how many visitors later became customers.

- You have to promote your site if you expect people to visit it.

- Ask visitors what they think of your site. If your customers would rather pick up the phone than use your site, you need to find out why.

- Cannibalization of existing sales channels isn't always as bad as it sounds. What is happening is actually a natural part of business evolution.

Defining the content

Armed with information regarding your site's goals and the primary audience, it's now time to start thinking about content. Although it's very tempting to start working on the structure itself (which looks very like an organization chart, but with subject headings instead of names of people), we need to know what type of information must be on the site before we start to put it into some kind of order. It's important to differentiate between the *type* of information and *actual* information. Here, we're only looking at types: in other words, we want to make note of the fact that we need to include information about "our XJ-140 Super Widget," but we probably don't need to start listing all its features yet. That's editorial content, which I'll talk a little more about in Chapter 11.

4.1 Information chunking

Information chunking simply means writing down each piece of information as it comes to mind so you don't forget something later on (Figure 4.1). It's useful to put each of these "chunks" on a separate file card or Post-it – or even a stack of napkins. This is what many of us did in the pre-computer days when researching a term paper: creating a separate file card for each source, quote, or other chunk of information.

There is no particular order in which this information is written down. Let's say we're going to work on a site designed to promote those wonderful handmade candles our friend Kate makes. Here are some of the chunks we may come up with:

- molded candles

- hand-dipped candles

- all-natural colors

- who is Kate?

- how to order

- the dipping process

- wax from own beehives

- candles make a wonderful home accent

- shipping charges
- Santa Claus candles for Christmastime

None of these is necessarily a category or menu title, the notes simply serve to remind us of something we think should eventually be represented on the site.

In companies that already have a stack of product brochures and catalogs, these are a natural source for checking the content (Figure 4.2). Make sure you go through them all fairly carefully.

Figure 4.1

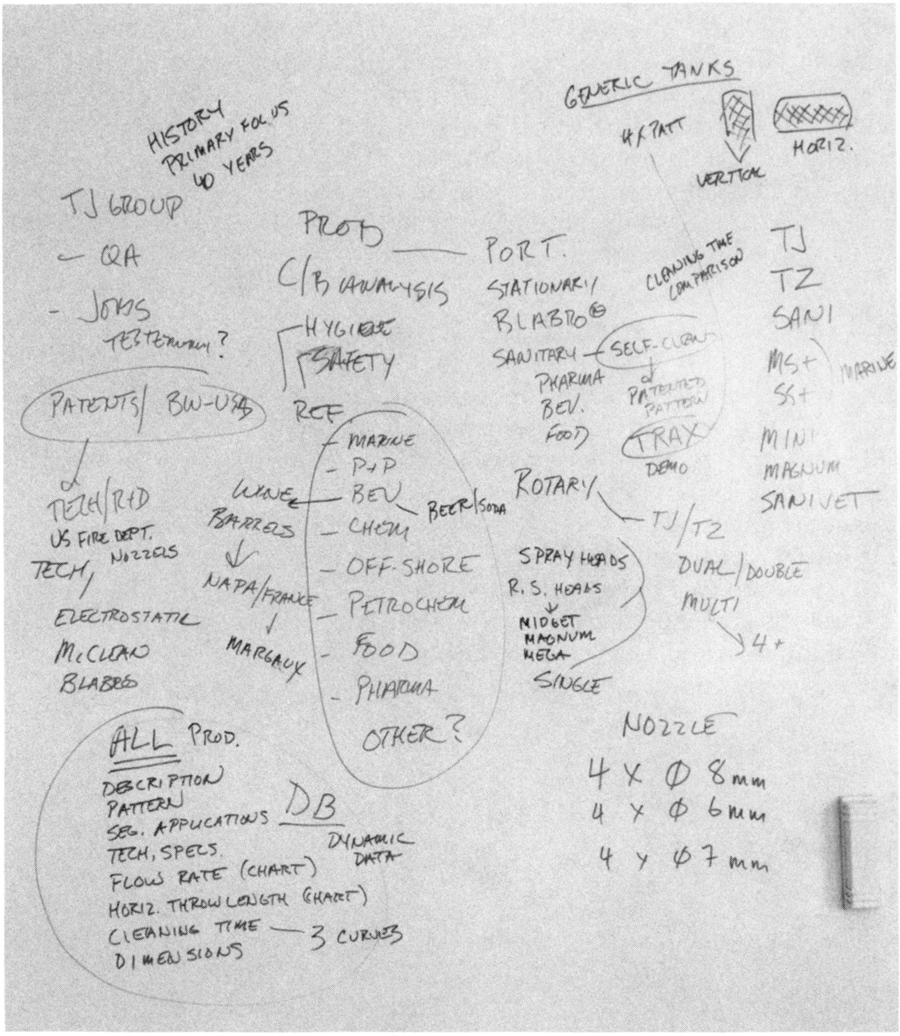

The typical result of a chunking session.

Figure 4.2   *Sorting through existing brochures and other printed material can help define content and suggest structural arrangements.*

4.2 Wish lists

If you're working in a group, it's very useful to have everybody create their own individual "wish list" of things they'd like to see on the site. You can also brainstorm ideas and write them up on a whiteboard, but often it's better to let people start out on their own, without being influenced by the others in the group. Later on, the lists can be compared and duplicate chunks can be eliminated.

That said, don't be too quick to discard similar, but not identical, chunks. For example, "international operations" may not be the same as "global operations." Make sure you talk these things through with whomever submitted the chunk so that you are clear as to the true definition. International operations could mean that the company participates in projects around the world. Global operations might mean that there are offices in 30 countries. These are two radically different pieces of information. It's also a hint to the information architect that when the time comes to label a menu item, visitors may also be confused as to the meaning of these words.

A structure starts to develop

When all the lists are displayed for the group, a chunk from one person will frequently inspire new chunks from others who hadn't previously thought about the subject. For example, one person may mention "unique technology" and someone else will add "patents" or some other related topic.

Invariably, subgroups of information will start to form, which will usually be reflected later on in the detailed structure. It helps to start keeping track of related items, particularly if the same basic information needs to be dealt with in different ways for different audiences. For example, if you're a paint manufacturer, "latex wall paints" will probably be presented differently when targeting professional painters (no harmful solvents) and homeowners (water-based for easy clean up). Make sure you note all the variations:

- latex wall paint (prof.)
- latex wall paint (home)

At this juncture, the web team usually splits up, and the information architect goes back to the office and tries to compile a single, consolidated list. A little more thought may go into what the information should be called (global, international, worldwide, etc.) but this is really work that will come later on.

It's not unusual to see the first information groupings starting to appear about now. This is very helpful as long as you don't commit yourself to informational groupings that will hinder your work later on. A word of warning: many teams think that precisely *because* these groups have been created, the structure is more or less in place. In truth, the process has a *long* way to go.

4.3 Role playing

When the list has been prepared, and perhaps refined a little, the information architect often goes back to the team in order to discover what other information may be missing. One of the most effective ways of doing this is to pretend that you're part of the target audience and attack the information as a visitor might.

For example, if one of your secondary goals is staff recruitment then examine the information as though you yourself were thinking of applying for a job. Is there an organizational chart? Are there definitions of job responsibilities within the individual departments? Is the employee handbook published on the site? (If you don't have one, do you *need* one?) Is there a pension plan? What about employee medical benefits? And more generally, are you, as a potential employee, getting an accurate impression of the corporate culture? Perhaps some actual employee testimonials would be useful.

Review every possible question a visitor within the defined audience could be expected to ask and make sure there's an answer somewhere. If no suitable chunk exists, add one; after all, that's the whole point of the exercise. When you've exhausted the possibilities, repeat the process for another target audience.

Here's an example of what happens when you *don't* ask the right questions. A few years ago, a leading car tire manufacturer went online with a very sophisticated and well-designed site. Visitors could indicate the year, make, and model of their car and the site would suggest suitable replacement tires – good news for all of us who haven't got a clue as to what size tires we need. Unfortunately, the site wouldn't recognize any car over three years old. Now honestly, how many people need new tires for a relatively new car? It took over a year before the site was finally updated to include older models; a clear indication that the site development team hadn't considered the questions the site's visitors could be expected to ask.

The only reason I ever returned to the site was out of professional interest – I had already bought new tires from another manufacturer. However, this goes to show that it can be dangerous to launch (or relaunch) a site too early, your visitors may never return to see all the wonderful improvements you've made. And don't even *think* about putting up "under construction" signs. Most of the users I've interviewed translate these to mean "launched and forgotten."

Retain your primary point of view

Role playing can be quite difficult for the site owner (the client) since there are usually many ingrained habits that are tough to break. If your primary viewpoint is that of a customer, for goodness sake don't forget that the customer's needs and understanding of the subject are not necessarily the same as those of your company. For example, a paint manufacturer may see paints as acrylic, vinyl, latex, epoxy, etc. However, customers may look at things from the point of view of use: indoor wall paint, outdoor paint for windows and trim, etc.

When chunking information, don't discard any particular information category just because another member of the team wants to create a different set of subgroups. For the moment, keep all your options open, although the goals of the site's *visitors* ought to dictate the final choice. Keep in mind that with several different user profiles, you may need unique groupings for each individual audience.

4.4 Reviewing competing websites

Examining other sites that are vying for the same audience isn't just useful, it's probably one of the most important research activities you can perform. This gives you an opportunity to see what sort of content others are providing and how they have chosen to group their information. In addition, looking at these sites will often give you clues as to what you should be calling things when the time comes to give your menus names, which is discussed in Chapter 10.

This process may also give you some ideas as to specialized online services you would like to incorporate that will help differentiate your site (more about this in the next chapter). That said, don't interpret this as an open invitation to steal good ideas from others. Remember, some online services and functions are based on patented technology which may prohibit their use, particularly in the United States.

Finally, make sure to refer back to these sites regularly. They, too, will probably be implementing improvements!

4.5 Teamwork or lonely nights?

In actual practice, it's usually easier for a well-briefed information architect to do the initial chunking in the privacy of his or her own office than to start from scratch at the first chunking session. However, "well-briefed" is the operative word. If you don't have a clue as to what a company does, you cannot contribute much beyond generic informational groups, products, sales and service, etc. This is why so many commercial website generators are able to produce reasonably functional opening menus – Microsoft FrontPage, for example, or Homestead.com, one of the better freebies on the web. On the other hand, if the architect has already worked closely with the site owner in some other way – for example, writing brochures, developing communication strategies, etc. – the chunks will have far greater value and can help the team "hit the ground running." This is also true if the people you are working with are novices since it's usually easier to build on (or tear down) something that already exists than to start from scratch.

Of course, some companies simply won't allocate the time needed for a group to work on a project, which means the information architect is forced to do the preliminary work in a vacuum – for better or for worse. By the way, one of the things that worries me most in my work as an information architect, is when a client has *no* comments whatsoever on a wishlist (or a full-blown structure) that I have developed on my own. If this happens to you, don't assume you've demonstrated a profound understanding of the needs of the company and their customers. Rather, take this as a sign that the others on the team probably aren't giving the process the attention it deserves!

Anyway, most web teams still benefit from creating their own initial wish lists, so if you've already done part of the chunking on your own, you might want to keep your list to yourself and use meeting times to coach those who are less familiar with the technique. You can always supplement their lists with your own items later on during team discussions.

Figure 4.3

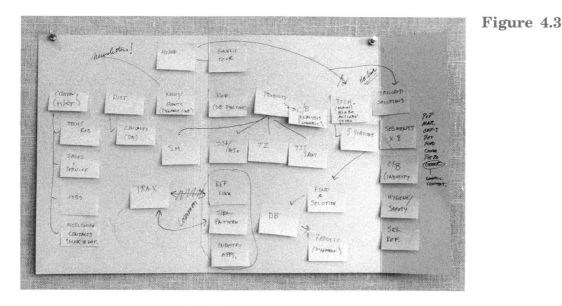

During the early stages of a web project, I often chunk and organize information in manila folders. Later on, if the site is particularly complex, I sometimes use a new folder for each individual main menu option.

4.6 The Post-it technique

If you are doing the work on your own, or are in a brainstorming session with just one or two others, the easiest way to collect the chunks is on small Post-its. It's easy to stick them on a wall, door, flipover chart, or even a big piece of cardboard. This lets you group and rearrange things as the process develops, and rename them when a more precise description comes to mind. The same Post-its are very useful later on when the time comes to start building the detailed structure.

Sometimes, a project of fairly modest size can be chunked and structured with Post-its stuck to the inside of a simple manila folder as shown in Figure 4.3. Don't laugh. It's convenient and can be tucked in a briefcase, and even worked on while sitting on a plane. In fact, some projects I've started in manila folders have eventually grown to become complex websites with hundreds of pages.

4.7 Process or outcome?

If you let the outcome (your goals) drive the information architecture process, you'll get there because you know where you're going. On the other hand, sometimes it's useful to let the *process* drive the outcome instead. You might just land somewhere much more exciting. For example, when Royal Dutch Shell set up their European sites, someone had the bright idea to provide a journey planner that allows visitors to create a customized map between any two European cities, conveniently marking all the Shell stations along the way. Even though the feature is very sophisticated and requires extensive daily maintenance, as a gimmick to get people to visit the site, it's worth its weight in gold! Take a look at www.ShellGeoStar.com (Figure 4.4). The message here is, keep track of all the bright ideas that pop up while you're chunking information or discussing the online services presented in the next chapter. You never know what might come in handy.

Keep in mind ...

- You need to identify *types* of content right now. Defining and generating the actual *editorial* content comes later.

- Create and compare individual wishlists or brainstorm content "chunks" as a group.

- Company literature can be a great source of inspiration.

- Even though informational groupings will start to appear, don't confuse these with the actual structure of the site.

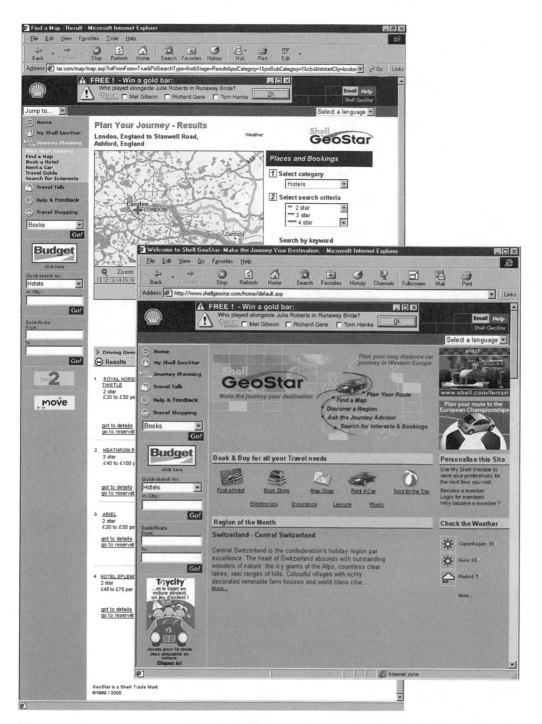

Figure 4.4 *The remarkable Shell GeoStar site provides detailed driving directions and maps between any two points in Europe – conveniently marking all Shell service stations along the route.*

- Don't automatically discard similar-sounding chunks – they may mean completely different things.

- Different target groups will usually need different types of information.

- Role playing can help you identify chunks that will be needed by specific audiences.

- Do some research. See what the web-based competition is up to!

- Save all your good ideas, even the wild ones. They may come in handy later on.

Providing useful services

The purpose of this chapter is to give you a little basic technical background so that you and your team can intelligently discuss the possibility of including special online features that will encourage visitors to come back again. It almost goes without saying that any meetings at which these services are discussed should be attended by your team's programmer or technical expert.

The fact is, virtually *no* business, web-based or otherwise, can survive without repeat sales. Your travel agent wants you to use their services each time you take a trip. Your supermarket wants you to buy your milk from them each and every week. Your car dealership wants you to come back every few years and buy a newer model. Moreover, the longer a product's lifetime, the more you want your customers to depend on *you* for parts and maintenance. Even if you're merely entertaining your visitors, you undoubtedly want them to come back sometime.

The features I'd like to talk about here often are a key ingredient in enhancing what we in the web-bizz call "the user experience."

5.1 User experience and online brand-building

In traditional print advertising, colors and logos are important when it comes to building a particular image for a product or company. These remain important considerations on the web, but not nearly as important as the overall user experience. That's because a website is an *application*. It's something people *use*, the same way they use a reference book, a word-processor, or a video game.

By default, a website becomes a product of your company, no matter how far removed it is from what you usually think of as your products or services. As such, the user experience must complement the image your company has built up in other media. Let's say, for example, that your products enjoy a reputation for ease of use. If your website, on the other hand, is extremely difficult to use, not only will your visitors take their business elsewhere, you may actually damage the overall market perception of your company. The people who claim that "all advertising is good advertising" simply don't know what they're talking about.

Remember, too, your website has to compete with similar products, rival websites. So, ask yourself, "What can *my* site do better than any of the others?" "What will make my site different?" In the advertising business, this is known as creating a "unique selling proposition" or "USP." I assure you, the position of your website in cyberspace vis-à-vis the competition is just as important as positioning any other product, brand, or service in traditional markets.

The battle for share of mind

Sales people are interested in market *share*: the percentage of the entire market for a particular product that actually uses your product rather than someone else's. This is usually measured in terms of sales volume or units shipped. More and more marketers, though, are interested in share of *mind*, which is difficult to measure even through customer surveys. What it means is that if your company enjoys a high share of mind, customers and potential customers think of *your* product or service before they think about your competitors. Customer awareness surveys show that share of mind and share of market are often closely related. However, I suspect the web is going to inspire a lot more research in this area. As opposed to market share, which is measured in terms of actual sales, a basic impression of share of mind can be gained by observing website statistics – the number of user sessions in particular.

5.2 Why people visit in the first place

Before we start trying to entice people to come *back* to your site, let's take a moment to analyze why people dropped by in the first place. Apart from those who surf in by mistake, most first-time visitors are:

- looking for a particular *type* of product, service, or information
- looking for a *specific* product, service, or piece of information
- merely curious to look at your site
    - because it turned up in a search
    - because another site suggested the link
    - because they know about your company for some other reason

The "other reason" mentioned in the last point could be one of many things. For example, the visitor might be a competitor who wants to check out your site. Of course, this person might also be a potential employee, or maybe they've dealt with your company before through other channels. Some people may have been inspired by a magazine article about your company or are responding to one of your own advertisements. "Curiosity," though, is the keyword in all of these cases.

At any rate, if the visitor is looking for something specific, your chances of winning a new customer are pretty good. For example, if you sell used books, the visitor probably searched for a specific title and came up with your site's listing. In other words, they didn't come to browse.

However, if visitors are just looking around, there's no guarantee they're actually out to buy something or are ready to deal with you in some other way. What this is leading up to is quite simple: you want these people to come back again and again.

5.3 Why people come back

But back to basics. The three fundamental reasons people come back are:

- to see if you have added new products or information,
- to investigate something they saw during an earlier visit,
- to use a service provided by the site itself.

Of course, people will often come back because your site is friendly, informative, helpful, or whatever – the same reasons people choose to shop in particular stores. Important as these issues are, they're still secondary considerations. After all, no one is going to go back to Kate's handmade candle site just because it's friendly – they're coming back because your website provides them with a convenient drive-up window. Convenience is probably the key ingredient when creating a positive user experience (although entertainment value can also be a big drawing card). So let's take a closer look at the above list.

The first point about looking for new products is more or less obvious: people go to book sites to see if their favorite author has published a new book, or to CD sites to browse through the latest releases, etc. As an information architect, keep in mind that you'll probably want to make it easy for people to discover the changes you've made since their last visit and locate related items and/or information (Figure 5.1). Section 13.7 discusses various ways to create "What's new" pages.

The second point, investigating something seen on a previous visit, is also obvious, but is frequently forgotten when personalizing a website according to past preferences. If a certain menu choice caught someone's eye the first time around, but the link wasn't followed, you may do more harm than good if you remove or relocate a menu option that you don't think a particular visitor is interested in. Remember, just because a visitor went in one direction on the first visit, there's no guarantee that he or she

Figure 5.1

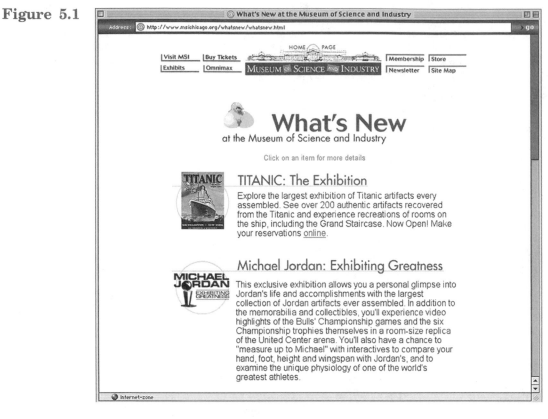

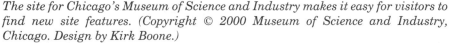

The site for Chicago's Museum of Science and Industry makes it easy for visitors to find new site features. (Copyright © 2000 Museum of Science and Industry, Chicago. Design by Kirk Boone.)

wants to take the same path the next time around. See Chapter 16 for more about personalization.

Which brings us to the third point, computer-assisted services. This is really the issue we're interested in right now since it can easily affect the basic thrust and structure of your site.

5.4 A review of basic computer capabilities

A note to technically minded readers

If you have some programming experience, the following sections will probably bore you to tears. Feel free to skim through the technical explanations to get to the examples.

And for everybody else

No one expects an information architect to be an expert in database design or any of the other subjects described on the following pages (though many professional information architects *are* experts). But it does help tremendously if you have a basic idea as to how computers think. After all, if you drive a car it's good to know how to fill up the gas tank and check the oil even if you're not a mechanic.

Don't worry about your lack of technical expertise; if your ideas are too far-fetched, I assure you, the programmers and system integrators on your team will be quick to let you know. There may also be hardware issues (usually related to performance) or software issues (usually related to the integration of legacy databases and customer relationship management tools) that will hinder the use of certain techniques. However, discussion of these is beyond the scope of this book.

A (very) short history of the computer revolution

In 1977, Ken Olsen, the founder and Chief Executive Officer of Digital Equipment Corporation is said to have remarked that there was no reason for anybody to have a computer in their home. His reaction to the first "home" computers raises a smile today but was actually quite reasonable at the time.

Back then, it was even difficult to convince the business community that there was a need for these machines since there were virtually no user applications. The launch of VisiCalc in 1979, the world's first spreadsheet program, changed all that and suddenly the pioneering Apple II had a legitimate business use. Soon after, Lotus 1-2-3 combined spreadsheet, database, and word-processing applications in a single integrated program to create a standard business tool for the IBM PC. Which brings us to the matter at hand, browser-based applications.

Although the range of applications for PCs has grown enormously since the late 1970s, it may come as a surprise to find that most computers still do what they've always done:

- make numerical calculations
- perform simple logical tasks
- store and retrieve information
- find and display specific pieces of information

The last item is actually linked to a database function (selective information retrieval), but this list is good enough for our present purposes. If possible (and if appropriate), we want to find out if we can create a browser-based application that will make your site more appealing and more useful to your target audience, thus encouraging them to place an order or come back again.

To inspire you, here are a few of the services others have successfully developed for their sites.

Numerical calculations   Generally speaking, if your company's consultants are asking your customers the same basic questions and then running back to the office to grab their pocket calculators, you can probably create a useful calculation tool. It's also fairly easy to combine a calculator function with a database from which supplementary information can be retrieved: interest rates, material costs, the price of tea in China, or whatever.

Dell Computers (www.dell.com) has a superb online store in which visitors can browse through the various basic models, choose the one they like best, and then use drop-down menus to customize various features

Figure 5.2

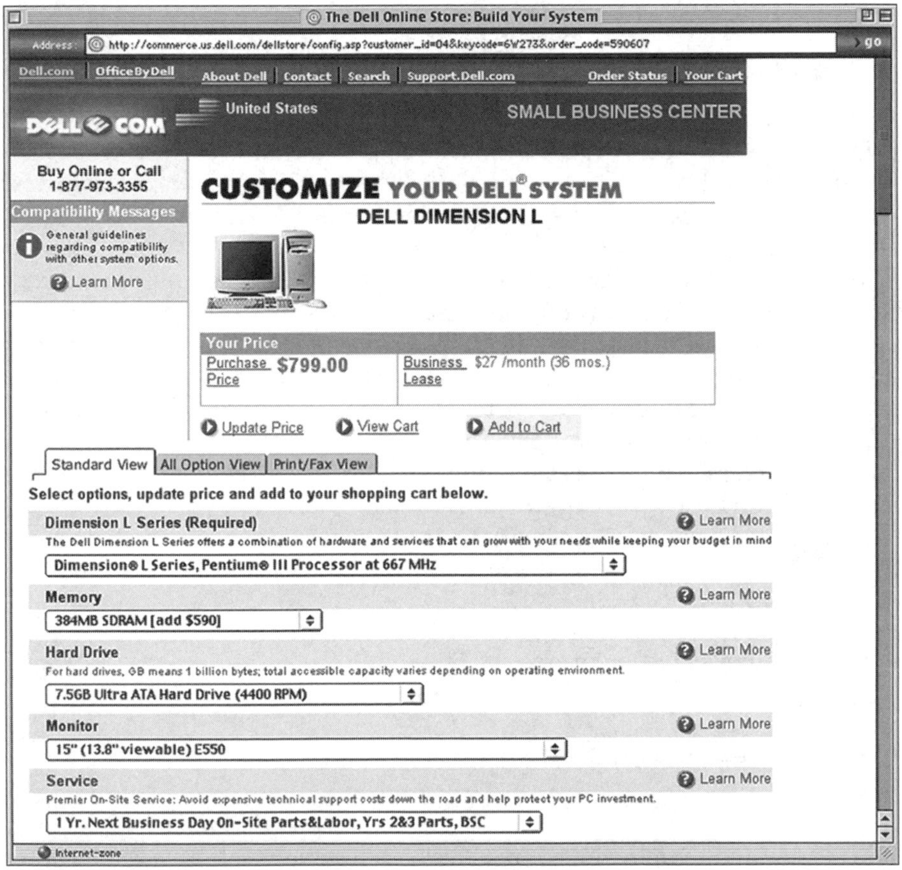

Dell helps potential buyers customize their new computer through numerous drop-down menus and then automatically calculates the price. When an order is placed, this information is forwarded directly to the people who will assemble the system. A first-rate example of sales and logistical integration.

(type of mouse, size of hard disk, etc.) as shown in Figure 5.2. The site application then adds up the cost of the modifications and immediately tells the visitor what the total price will be. After an order is placed, this information is sent directly to the people who put together the computer – a very effective business model in which the website functions as a key link in the supply chain.

Many banks are now using their general-access websites to help people calculate the costs of personal loans and mortgages. Although few institutions have actually gone so far as to *approve* loans online, more and more banks are at least giving online visitors an initial approval based on the credit and financial information that has been submitted. This helps weed out the bad risks and encourages the rest to pay a personal visit. That said, several web banks now specialize in transactions that are 100 percent browser-based – there are no offices! Assuming they can create the degree of trust needed to woo customers from bricks-and-mortar organizations, there's no doubt they'll eventually figure out how to provide *all* the services of a traditional financial institution.

Of course, you don't have to be a bank to provide visitors with a useful online service. Rockwool A/S, a Danish-based producer of firesafe insulation, has put together a special application in which homeowners can submit information about their house (size, number of floors, type of roof, etc.), the type of heating (oil, gas, or electric), and other basic data (see Figure 5.3). The application then makes a calculation based on the specific input combined with local fuel costs. In just a few clicks, the visitor learns how much it will cost to properly insulate the house and the expected payback time in terms of lower heating costs.

Unfortunately, this service is not yet on any of the English-language Rockwool sites, but it certainly *ought* to be. It's a very good idea and firmly establishes the company as experts in their chosen field. And think, would you do the calculations on the Rockwool site and then go out and buy a competing product? Probably not.

Performing logical tasks   A decision tree is a simple structure that asks questions (usually yes/no) to steer you towards the right solution. Figure 5.4 shows an absurdly simple decision tree designed to help you choose between three products that all perform the same basic function.

Programmers call this kind of sorting "binary recursive partitioning" using IF/THEN Boolean operators as the underlying logic for the system – IF "Yes" THEN "Product B". Decision trees are the subject of many doctoral dissertations and are not always easy to design. Happily, that's not our job. What we really want to know is if we can use this technique to help our site's visitors.

In many instances, a visitor may be interested in a particular type of product, but doesn't know which one to choose. By asking specific questions, such as those described in our simple model, the decision tree can be used to make appropriate recommendations.

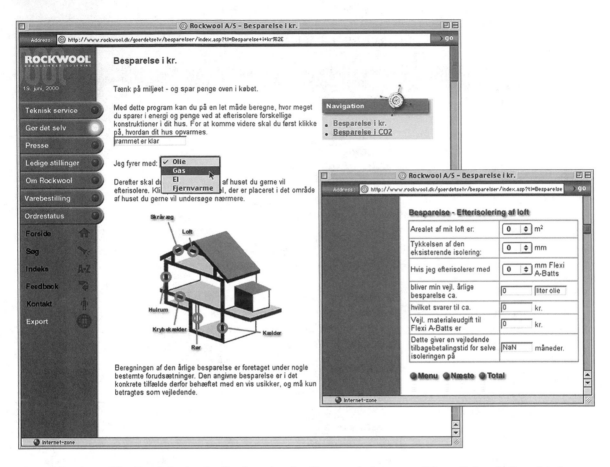

Figure 5.3 *The Danish site for Rockwool, a leading manufacturer of firesafe insulation, lets home-owners calculate the payback time for their project in terms of reduced heating cost. The visitor is asked to indicate the current method of heating (oil, gas, electricity, district heating) and answer a few simple questions regarding any of six areas of their house that they may want to insulate.*

Back in 1992, one of the first interactive projects featuring a true graphic interface that I was involved with was a program designed to present a range of sophisticated flowmeters (Figure 5.5). These are devices that measure the amount of liquid that passes through a pipe at a particular point; residential water meters are simple flowmeters. Finding the right product depended on some fancy arithmetic based on the user's specific needs (pipe dimensions, etc.). The computer asked the user to type in eight numerical parameters, did the calculations needed, and used the results to answer questions contained in its internal decision tree. At the touch of a button, the computer displayed the flowmeter that was best suited to the job – a complicated task that used to take trained engineers about 20 minutes to complete.

Figure 5.4

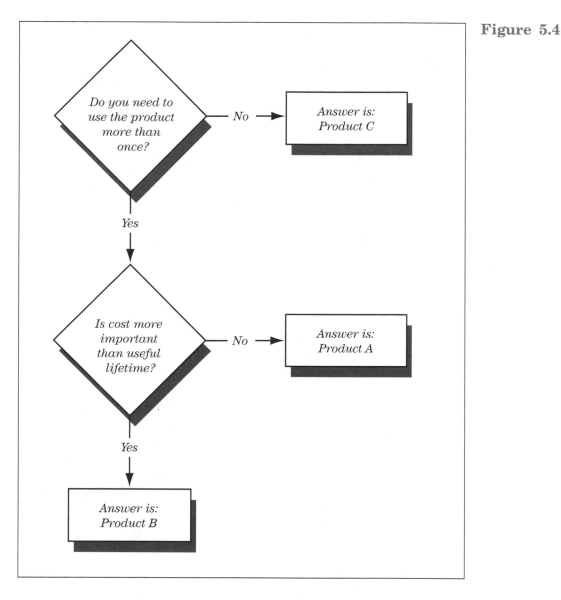

This simple decision tree helps users choose between three products that all perform the same basic function. Product A features long lifetime and higher cost. Product B features short lifetime and lower cost. Product C is an inexpensive, single-use disposable.

In the previous example, the potential flowmeter customer had a specific problem that needed to be solved and wanted a straightforward answer. It would have been unreasonable to ask them to plow through page after page of technical specifications in order to find what they were looking for.

Figure 5.5

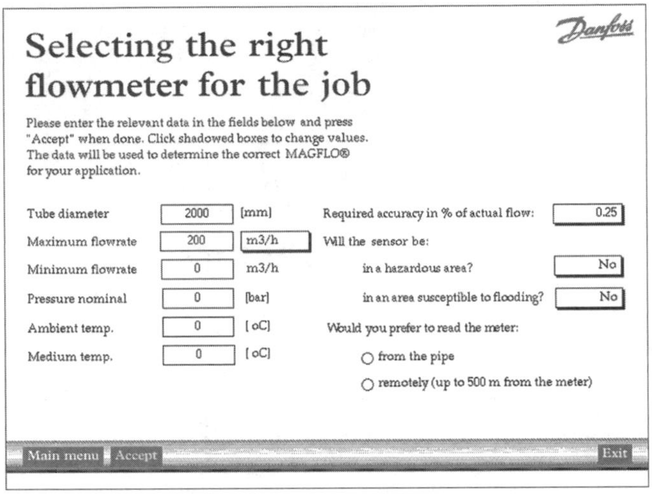

This diskette-based program, dating from the early 1990s, helped increase aware-ness of the company and its products by 40 percent in the European market. The product configurator was a tremendously popular feature that enabled users to perform a complicated task in less than a minute.

Storing and retrieving information   This is about databases: collections of well-defined information that can be examined, categorized, and retrieved as needed. Although most of us use a database of one sort or another in the course of our daily work, I've discovered that very few people actually know how a database works. Since information architects *should* know, here's a quick explanation.

Imagine for a moment a desk drawer. Most of us just dump in our pencils, pens, loose change, whatever to create one big mess. The more organized among us will divide the drawer up into smaller sections so their pens are in one place, pencils another, and so on. A database is like a huge chest of drawers, each drawer with its own set of identical compartments for pens, pencils, etc.

A typical database consists of a number of "fields" or *types* of information relating to a single subject (individual compartments). For example, if we were going to build a product database, the product name might be located in one field, the descriptive text in another, a product number in the third, and a photo might be indicated by a fourth field (Figure 5.6). The entire collection of related fields is called a "record" (the whole drawer). As you may have gathered, fields can contain numbers, letters, or even graphics. Moreover, you can have any number of fields in your database depending on your particular needs. The individual data contained in the fields are *attributes* or *metadata* that relate specifically to the record in question.

Figure 5.6

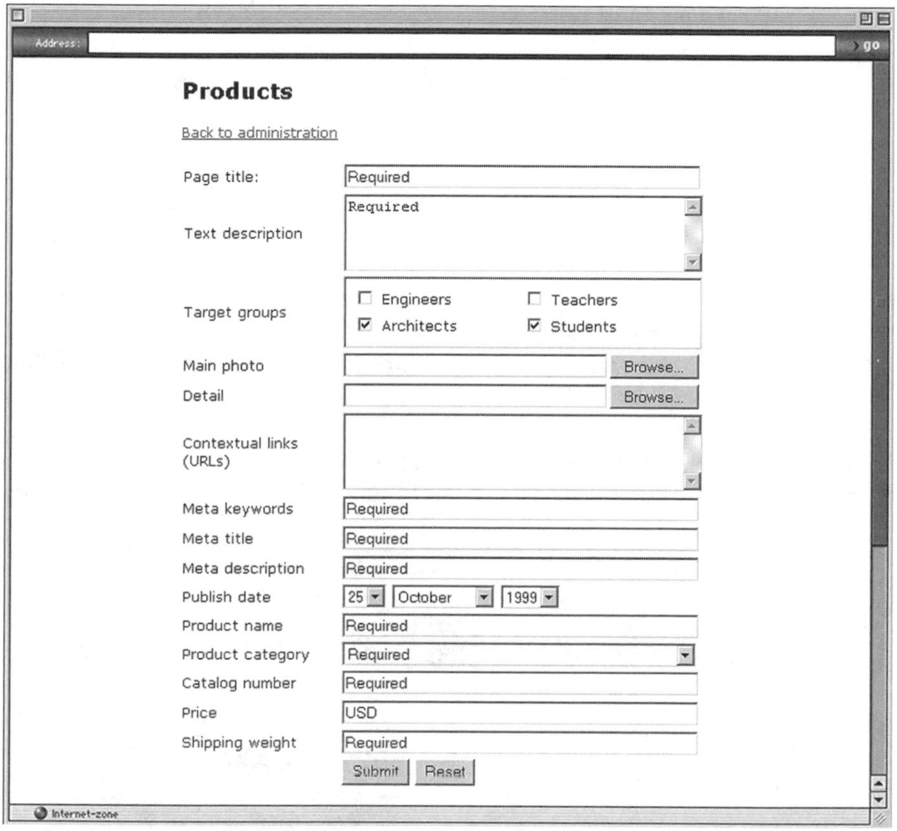

A content-management screen from an administrative interface indicating the various database fields for a typical product.

A card catalog at a library is probably one of the best known databases. Each record contains three fields: author, title, and subject. "William Shakespeare" would be an author attribute.

So now that you know how databases are put together, let's take a look at some practical uses when creating a website. For example, if your site contains a large number of pages with similar *types* of content, such as books, CDs, impressionist paintings, or whatever, registering information in a database can make life easier for yourself as well as your user. Information architecture professionals call this type of content "structured, homogeneous information." At any rate, by tapping into your database, your site can be programmed to automatically generate pages containing the specific information requested by a visitor. The site simply pours data (attributes) from the relevant database fields into a standardized layout. The big advantage of this technique is that the site is much simpler to maintain since a change in the basic layout only needs to be made once instead of on hundreds (or thousands) of separate pages. Also, it's generally easier (and a lot safer) to get content providers to update a database (using a special content-management interface) rather than letting them fool around with the site directly.

Remember that a database is a *technique* rather than a feature in itself. As such, it's almost always of more use to the site owner than to the site visitor. It's like the old story about someone who buys an electric drill at the hardware store. They don't actually want a *drill*, what they really want is a *hole*. So let's drill some holes.

Finding and displaying relevant information   The single most important advantage of a database is that it facilitates the identification of information that's interesting and, by default, eliminates information that isn't. This is pretty much what a search engine does when it sets out to find something.

Many sites have created useful customization features that tap into categorized information stored in databases. For example, CNN.com

Figure 5.7

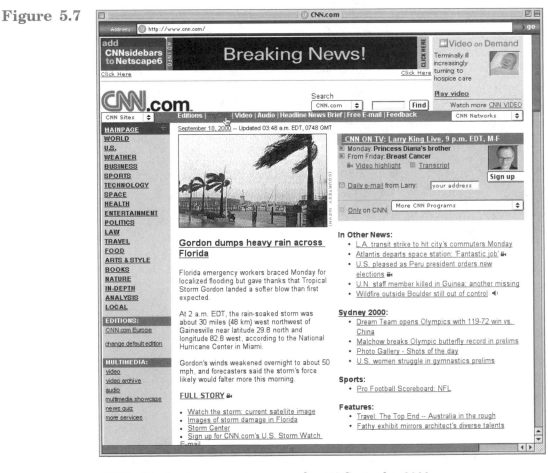

CNN's standard screen as it appeared on 18 September 2000.

(Figure 5.7) lets visitors create their own customized homepage by defining what they are interested in and what they aren't (Figure 5.8). One user may choose to see all the news about, say, health care without having their page cluttered up with unwanted stories about home improvements. Someone else may want to focus on politics, air travel, and classic movies.

This is also how Amazon.com puts together those clever recommendation lists. Since the site already knows what you're interested in – because you've told it what you like and don't like to read when you signed up for the service, and Amazon "remembers" what books you've purchased in the past – the site simply searches its database and picks out books in similar genres, by the same authors, or on the same subjects. In addition, it compares your purchases with those of other customers with similar interests. As a result, some of their purchases will also show up on your recommendation list (you'll find more information about this in Chapter 16).

Figure 5.8

The myCNN screen, customized according to my personal preferences, also from 18th September.

More about user-defined content   Some online museums enable visitors to create custom exhibitions by coupling a database with a search-like facility that eliminates unwanted items. For example, art museums use certain basic parameters to categorize and display their holdings: period (Renaissance, Modern, etc.); nationality (Italian, Flemish, French); style (Impressionist, Cubist, etc.); and so on. But in the virtual world, a site could let visitors define their own categories so they could view German portraits, landscapes painted in 1847, or even just those paintings that are mostly blue. It's simply a question of how much detailed information you're willing to put into the database. So, you may not be interested in art, but keep this feature in mind if you're out to build some other site in which the same basic information must be rearranged and catagorized according to individual needs. For instance, just think how many car parts are identical on different models from the same manufacturer.

On a related note, because the technology of the internet is ideal for making direct product comparisons, many sites now make it possible to compare two or more products on the basis of specific parameters using selective retrieval methods. For example, someone looking for a new dishwasher for their kitchen may be interested in comparing the noise levels of the various models, or perhaps the water consumption. The Weber barbecue site does this very well, comparing the features for any three of their many backyard grills (www.weber.com). Click on "Grills and accessories" and then "Compare models" (Figure 5.9).

Some sites are entirely database-driven, permitting the visitor to dive directly into the information he or she wants. The limitation, though, is that people don't always know what they're looking for, which can sometimes make these search-type sites very difficult to use. The most useful database-driven sites draw extensively on a *controlled vocabulary*. Here, people choose subjects from pre-determined lists rather than typing in random keywords which may or may not be defined in the database. For example, the term "International" may be defined in the controlled vocabulary so the database doesn't also have to understand the terms "Global" and "Worldwide."

Forums and chat rooms   In essence, a forum is simply a page (or collection of pages) on a site on which visitors can post e-mail-type comments regarding some subject of common interest. These are also called "bulletin boards" or "newsgroups."

Sometimes, the site owner will provide a few "seeded topics" to get things rolling – topics posted and initially responded to by the site owner him- or herself. The basic idea is to create a knowledge bank from which visitors can gain experience and exchange relevant information regarding a specific subject or problem.

Chat rooms are similar except that they usually feature live, online discussions, often at fixed times. During these sessions, everyone in the

Figure 5.9

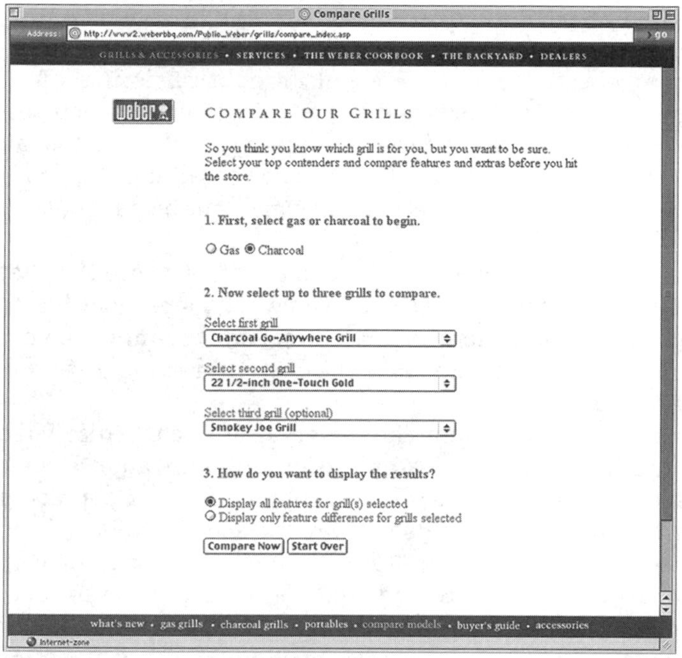

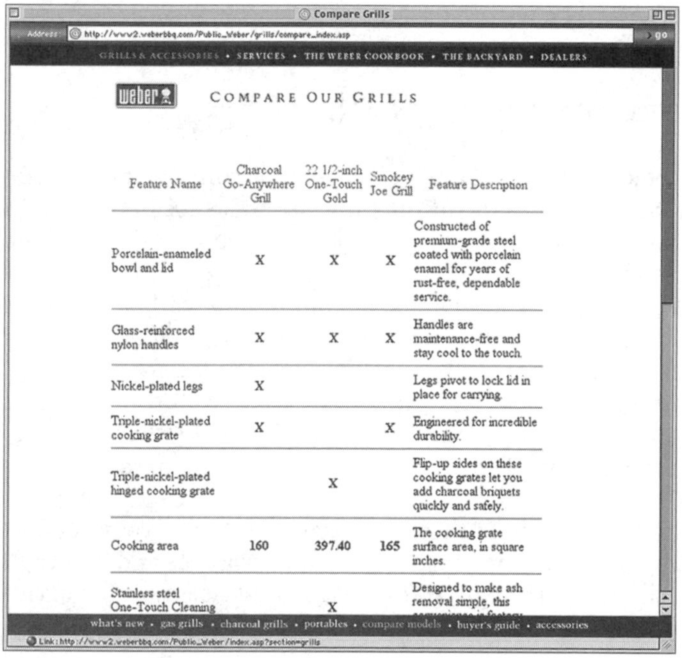

The Weber barbecue site lets visitors compare the features of up to three different gas or charcoal grills – a great convenience for budding backyard chefs.

chat room can see and respond to any comments posted by other visitors. Generally, live chats are reserved for people who want to discuss a particular hobby (stamp collecting, etc.), personal or political issues (drug abuse, up-coming elections, etc.), or are just out to socialize (dating services, etc.). As transfer speeds on the internet improve, and webcams fall in price, we'll soon be able to *see* the people we're talking to also – although removing some of a visitor's anonymity may not be particularly welcomed.

Businesses rarely feature live chats except in situations where the chat room functions as part of a help-desk service. Generally, a product has to have a very large user base (Microsoft Windows, for example) before enough site traffic can be generated to make the chat interesting. After all, it's no fun talking to yourself.

On the other hand, technical forums can be very useful, particularly if a product is subject to a high degree of customization: software applications, for example. In this case, programmers can exchange tips and chunks of code with one another to solve problems that are too specific to have been covered in the normal documentation. Alternatively, a business may choose to target a particular audience and create a special forum to serve this audience's needs. For example, a window manufacturer might create a special design forum for architects (new buildings) or contractors (renovations).

5.5 Make your product the "hero"

The three primary colors, blue, red, and yellow, can be combined in an infinite number of ways to create an infinite number of colors. You might think about the three basic computer functions, calculation, logic, and storage/retrieval, as the primary colors of computer programming.

The examples you've just read are not a comprehensive list nor were they meant to be. They are included merely to give you an idea as to the kinds of things you can accomplish if you understand and take advantage of the computer's basic abilities. Ask yourself, "What would my visitors like to do while they're on my site? What problems do they want to solve?" And most important of all, "How can I help them reach these objectives?"

Whatever you do, you *must* maintain your basic focus, and your product should always remain the hero of your site. The online services and functions you choose to add should *further the sales process* and not merely provide some entertaining diversion. Your goal should be *flows*, not *features*.

Keep in mind ...

- A website is an *application*, and as such, it is a product of your company.
- The *user experience* is the key to online brand building.

- Find out what your site needs to do *better* than any of the competing websites out there. What is your site's unique selling proposition?

- Give your visitors a good reason to come back. Like most brick-and-mortar organizations, your site will probably need repeat business to survive.

- Today's computers do pretty much what they have always done: make numerical calculations, perform logical tasks, store and retrieve information.

- How you *use* these capabilities is what makes an online service unique and worthwhile to your visitors.

- Ask yourself, "How can I help my visitors reach *their* objectives?"

- Make sure your product remains the "hero" of your site.

6 Ensuring successful online sales

An incredible amount has been written on the subject of e-commerce, "Own the customer's total experience" and other marketing hype. However, for most "e-tailers," the rules of selling anything on the web are pretty much the same as they are anywhere else. For instance, if your website provides friendly service through convenient architecture, intuitive navigation, pleasing visual design, and an appropriate tone of voice, albeit written, the greater the chance your visitors will browse and buy.

Although the list of things you can do to make your site more appealing, practical, and informative is long, there are two basic requirements a site *must* meet if you expect people to buy your product online. These are:

- build shared references
- establish trust

Many of the techniques described here will first be put into practice during the design phase or when gathering editorial content. However, they also provide inspiration for the information architect when structuring the site. As such, the sooner you know about them the better. Let's take a closer look.

6.1 Building shared references

Quite simply, a shared reference is something that is totally familiar to two different people. For example, if you mention a McDonald's Big Mac, most Americans will know exactly what you're referring to. If you call an Apple computer dealer and tell them you need a replacement mouse for your blueberry iMac, they'll know exactly what you want because you *share* a point of reference. If you thought "blueberry" was a fruit, you're probably a PC user – and thus lack the shared reference.

Shared references are reassuring and are often the key to any kind of successful long-distance sales transaction. A good printed mail-order catalog will provide a concise written description of each available item for this very reason. If a shared reference with the target audience can (to some extent) be assumed, such as a standard computer mouse, the written description may be all that is needed. However, if there is uncertainty with regard to the degree of shared reference, for example, a special ergonomic mouse, a photograph or diagram will help tremendously. Without it, the potential buyer faces uncertainty and may hesitate to place an order. This is one of those instances where a picture can really be worth a thousand words. With the exception of brand-name jeans, most of us wouldn't dream of buying clothes without at least having seen a photo.

Putting things in perspective (literally)

Products that vary greatly in size, such as industrial vacuum cleaners, do well to include a human model in the photo (as shown in Figure 6.1). This immediately conveys a sense of size, and is often a far more useful indicator than a technical drawing. Expecting a potential buyer to refer to a detailed drawing is probably asking more than one should, although ideally, both references should be available. By the way, if a product is totally unique, a photo sends a strong signal to the visitor that the product actually exists (although we've all seen lots of mock-ups).

Figure 6.1

Potential customers for this Nilfisk-Advance ID 2050 industrial vacuum cleaner are left with no doubt as to the physical size of the machine thanks to the human model.

Figure 6.2

Read this description, picture the bulb in your mind, and then turn the page ...

25W novelty lightbulb. Clear glass with standard E27 base. Pink and green filament lights up with "I Love You" message.

... and figuratively

Amazon.com has solved the problem of letting readers "thumb through a book" by allowing people who have read a book to post their personal comments online. Seeing what other people think about the book often gives you a pretty good idea as to what to expect when your own copy arrives. Moreover, quite a few of Amazon's non-fiction titles feature an online table of contents, which is tremendously useful if you're looking for information on a very specific topic that you think might be found in a book with a more general title. More recently, Amazon has even started to show sample pages.

Three-dimensional, user-controlled graphics are still in the experimental stage and have yet to gain widespread usage. However, it's reasonable to assume that some day soon, we will be able to pick up and "handle" products using some sort of virtual reality interface. The whole idea, though, is to create a shared reference, "Here, look at what I have. Is this what you want?"

The shared-reference test

Assuming a shared reference that does not really exist is perhaps the single greatest mistake one can make when putting together an e-commerce site. Stated bluntly, don't take *anything* for granted! If you're in doubt, pick up the phone, call someone, and describe a common object – a light bulb, for example (see Figure 6.2). Then have them ask you questions about it that can be answered with a simple yes or no. If you answer "no" to anything, your description failed the shared reference test. For example, if the person you're talking to asks if the bulb is frosted, but you actually had a clear bulb in mind, you now know that you need to revise

Figure 6.3

Was this what you expected to see? Probably not. The written description on the previous page, although accurate, wasn't enough to create a shared reference.

your description accordingly. You may be surprised at how many things you forgot to mention! Although much of this is related directly to specific editorial content, it's up to the information architect to make sure that the site structure provides a logical point of inclusion for any written or graphic elements that will be needed later on in order to create this reference.

6.2 Establishing trust

E-commerce is like any other sales venture, there has to be an atmosphere of mutual trust. Most of us wouldn't hesitate to phone a major department store and ask them to send us something (if we have a shared reference to draw on). We know these institutions to be honest, service-minded, and efficient. We also know that they'll honor our credit card. Mutual trust is the key.

Websites, though, don't have fancy buildings. They can appear one day and disappear the next. For unknown companies, people must be taught to trust the site itself, since this is all that is visible. There are several ways to do this.

A few common tricks of the trade

The most basic ingredient in creating trust is to supply the site visitor with reassuring background information: a well-thought-out "About the company" page, for example. Granted, the page may be one long lie, but to leave out the page altogether is a mistake nonetheless. False advertising legislation for the internet still has a long way to go before it becomes effective, which is why some site owners who provide multivendor e-commerce services, such as online auction houses, often require users to sign electronic contracts in which people agree to stand by their words.

Another tactic is to eliminate any risk on the part of a potential purchaser. For example, many software houses let you download their software for free, so-called "trialware." The download is generally locked in some way so that it only functions for a limited time (enough to try things out and make a decision), or lacks certain functions (a word-processing program that won't let you print, for example). In either case, if the user wants to keep the software, a password "key" to unlock the program is supplied upon receipt of payment.

Money-back guarantees are always useful, but these cannot be relied on heavily if you have not already created some basic degree of trust. Moreover, sending things back and forth always costs money, which is usually the responsibility of the purchaser, even if the item is returned.

Figure 6.4

The testimonial at the top provides a strong incentive to read more about this remarkable product and download the free trial version. If you want to improve your search engine ratings, this offer is hard to resist!

Reference customers are one of the best ways in which an unknown company can create an atmosphere of trust. References help prove that the company has actually done what they say they can do – and, if appropriate, even explain how they did it.

Actual testimonials from past customers are very reassuring to those people who are still in doubt (Figure 6.4). For example, if you're out to buy a computerized backgammon game and a testimonial from a former national champion says, "It's the best backgammon program I've ever used," you'll probably feel you've found the right product. Naturally, there's no guarantee that the former champion has ever tried other programs, but that's the age-old problem of all testimonials.

The eBay feedback system

Pierre Omidyar, founder of eBay online auctions (www.ebay.com), pioneered a tremendously effective feedback system in which both sellers and buyers are encouraged to say a few words about how the transaction worked out (see Figure 6.5). Positive, negative, and neutral comments are

Figure 6.5

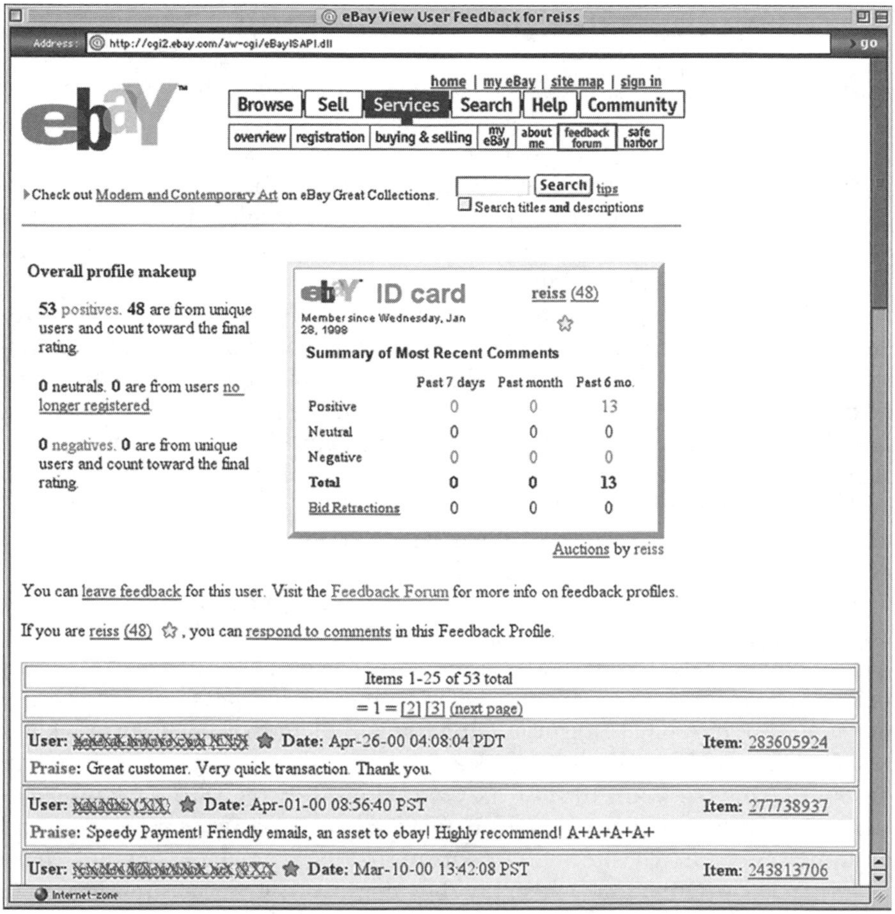

eBay's tremendously successful feedback system serves to create trust between two private individuals who have never met. This happens to be a page of feedback about me. I figure that if one works in the web industry, it helps to have personal as well as theoretical e-commerce experience.

allowed. Negative feedback is taken very seriously and eBay reserves the right to reject users who have received more than three negative comments. The feedback system has proved so useful, some sellers will now send items to highly-rated purchasers *before* they've even received payment. Remarkably, eBay has succeeded in creating trust between two private individuals who have never met, yet often exchange hundreds of dollars without hesitation. This is the level of trust that every e-commerce site should strive for.

Keep in mind, *if people don't trust your site, how can you expect them to trust your product?*

6.3 Keep the sales process moving

Although this next section deals strictly with functional issues, again, it is a subject that will also influence the decisions made by the information architect. That's why it's included here.

When browsing through a website, users are often asked to e-mail for a catalog, brochure, or other information This is annoying because the site owner has clearly not bothered to think about *why* someone happens to be using the medium in question.

The web has a "here-and-now" immediacy and when we visit a site, we do so voluntarily. In other words, we've made a conscious effort to go somewhere specific in the hopes of finding information *now*, not tomorrow or next week. The fact is, most websites that want us to e-mail for a brochure or price list could have saved us all both time and trouble by putting this stuff on their site to begin with – food for thought for budding information architects. Personally, I object to having to download Adobe Acrobat PDF files even though the response time is less than an e-mail request. I'd much rather be able to browse through this information directly on the website, where it has hopefully been edited so that I get right to the facts without any of the narrative that usually pads out a printed brochure.

Remember, too, that by the time someone has reached the point at which he or she is interested in a pricelist, the chances are, they're already thinking about buying something or making a specific comparison. Clearly, this is *not* the time to hinder the sales process by forcing an e-mail request. In traditional terms, we want to *close the sale*. Moreover, by asking for information, many sites put visitors on the defensive by whisking away their shroud of anonymity – and visitors often end up asking: "Do I really want these people to know who I am?" (Usually they do not – not yet, at any rate.)

Always keep in mind *anything that diminishes the here-and-now aspect of the web will often have a negative influence on the visitor*.

On a related note, make sure you always provide feedback, both in the form of a special "Thank you" screen to acknowledge the receipt of the order, as well as a detailed e-mail that can function as a receipt. Also, depending on who your customers are, you may also need to make arrangements to accept purchase orders in addition to other forms of payment. A second e-mail when the order has actually been sent is a good idea too. In fact, more sophisticated sites actually allow customers to track the entire ordering process, which is particularly useful if a waiting period is involved due to stock shortages or other delays.

6.4 Keep it simple for users

Although this really has more to do with site usability than site structure, many online shops make it extremely difficult for a visitor to actually order a product. Sometimes, a separate e-mail message is requested, which

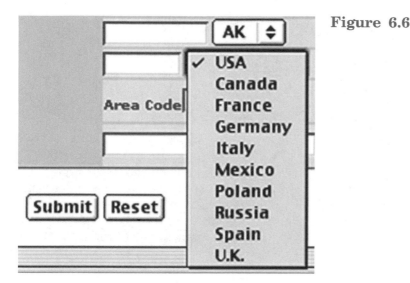

Figure 6.6

Since I live in Denmark, this extremely limited (and somewhat odd) range of response options prevented me from completing my online transaction. I had to e-mail the webmaster instead – most people would simply have taken their business elsewhere.

is fine for high-priced collectables and other unique items. On the other hand, some sites require visitors to fill out complicated forms, which then have to be printed and faxed to the company. Even worse, a long online form may simply not work or insist on information that cannot be supplied by the user (Figure 6.6). A good example of this is the "state/province" field that most online forms include as part of the address information. Many countries outside North America have no state or province as part of the standard address. Living in Denmark, as I do, this is a daily irritation and I am often forced to fill in some nonsensical answer before I'm allowed to submit my information. In the worst cases, I've simply been forced to give up and take my business elsewhere.

If you expect people to purchase several different items from you during a single online session, an electronic shopping cart is an absolute necessity. Not only do you make it easy for your visitors, the shopping cart also makes it possible to record a lot of secondary information on the order sheet that is useful for you but would be inconvenient for the customer to supply, shipping weight, for example.

6.5 Objections to online sales

If, for the most part, you only serve a single national market, you'll probably want to just skim the rest of this chapter and go on to the next. And for everyone else ...

Many international organizations are reluctant to initiate online sales for any or all of the following reasons:

- prices vary from market to market
- prices vary from customer to customer
- not all products are available in all markets
- they don't want to cannibalize existing market channels

The last point was discussed in Chapter 2, so I won't repeat the arguments here (not without a hyperlink). Suffice to say that the key reason for using the web is that it provides a *new* market channel, and is not necessarily a replacement for existing channels. As far as the other issues are concerned, I cannot claim to have a simple answer to any of them, but there are a few points your team should consider.

Different prices from market to market

If your company has manufacturing facilities in several different countries, local labor costs will invariably affect the net sales price of a particular item. Other issues include sales tax or value-added tax, plus import duties, all of which vary tremendously from market to market. In addition, fluctuating exchange and interest rates may be a contributing factor. Finally, your company may have cut prices in a particular country in order to gain market share. Here are some of the ways companies are working around these problems.

Reducing labor costs   If labor costs *are* an issue because similar products are produced in several different countries, many companies have re-adopted the old "FOB" pricing principle. FOB stands for "free on board" and represents the price of an article, excluding local and/or national tariffs, delivered to a particular location. For example, a kitchen blender made in Europe that is priced "FOB Copenhagen" means that the article's price would not include 9 percent import duties on small electrical appliances, 25 percent Danish VAT and other surcharges. This price may well be higher than a similar blender made in Korea and sold "FOB Seoul" because European labor costs are generally higher than those in the Far East. However, the purchaser at least gets an indication of what something will cost and can order intelligently online having factored in the applicable transportation costs.

Reducing local tariffs   If labor costs are not an issue, one solution to the problem is to calculate the base price of an article, excluding any local tariffs, shipping charges, etc. Price differences from market to market should be negligible.

Reducing exchange rates   The truth is, exchange and interest rates will *always* be a factor, no matter what you do. One of the key advantages of the euro (€) is that it reduces the need to factor in exchange rates within a large part of the European Union (EU). That said, exchange rates between Europe, the Americas and Asia will continue to be an issue.

In most instances, international companies simply transfer their normal export pricing practices to the web, often using a pricelist in a single major currency, such as US dollars. If nothing else, web-based pricelists are easier to update, which can sometimes be a big advantage.

Prices vary from customer to customer

Important customers may enjoy price reductions due to the size of their orders. For example, a professional contractor will undoubtedly pay less for house paint than I will as a private individual. One solution is simply to ask special customers to inquire about quantity or professional discounts; although in practice, a major customer will probably *not* be dealing with you online unless you've taken the trouble to create special transaction-based sites for your key customers. This is, of course, the most useful long-term solution.

If a company has cut prices in a particular market in order to gain sales volume, in most cases, they're really admitting that they can live with lower margins. Moreover, since the web cuts out the middleman, online products generally have higher profit margins to begin with.

Price-setting according to what the individual markets will bear is something of a balancing act for most international organizations, and I suspect that the advent of the internet will eventually make this practice obsolete. In fact, savvy international customers have always shopped around if they thought they could get a bargain in another market. Here's an interesting example.

Some years ago, one of my clients lowered prices locally in order to penetrate a South American market. A US company discovered this and immediately started placing orders south of the equator rather than dealing with the local distributor just down the street. As the products were sent directly from Europe, shipping costs were not an issue. The upshot of all this is: the American customer continues to get products at a discounted price; the South American distributor scores a nice profit simply by sending off an e-mail to company headquarters; the American distributor, who did all the sales groundwork, is completely out of the loop (and none too pleased about it); and the European manufacturer is now discounting products in a market that used to be willing to pay a higher price. Mind you, all this happened *before* they went online. I'll let you draw your own conclusions as to what the future holds.

Not all products are available in all markets

Product availability is always an issue when products have to be approved for use by various local authorities before they can be sold. For example, in the United States, electrical devices must be UL-approved; within the European Union, they must be CE-approved. Sometimes products, particularly medical devices, are approved for certain uses in one country and for other uses in another. Pharmaceuticals may be over-the-counter one place and prescription-only elsewhere.

If you're not out to actually hide the fact that you produce different products for different markets, the easiest solution is simply to ask the visitor up front in which country the company's products will be used – or at least delivered. It's then possible to customize the site (using a database) to exclude products that are illegal or simply unavailable. Some sophisticated sites link to local subsites which only present locally available products. However, this solution can get messy if the local site doesn't duplicate all of the basic corporate information found on the main site. In some instances, the language of the site may actually jump from English to a local language and back again, which is incredibly disconcerting.

I realize that these brief remarks only touch the tip of a very large iceberg. Nevertheless, over the next few years, these issues will become extremely important as prices become more transparent, thus reducing their usefulness in terms of penetration strategy. At least this gives you some idea as to the decisions you'll be facing in the near future.

Keep in mind ...

- You need to establish shared references in order to sell anything online.

- You also need to establish trust. People won't trust your products if they don't trust your site.

- Conduct a simple shared-reference test if you are ever in doubt about a product description.

  Keep the sales process moving. Don't stop things by asking people to send you an e-mail or write for a printed catalog.

- Make it as easy as possible for people to order items online.

- The web is a *new* market channel, not necessarily a replacement for existing channels.

- If your company objects to online sales, make sure to re-evaluate your position on a regular basis. The web has a faster pace than you might think.

Deciding on the type of site

During the initial goal-setting phase, your web team will probably have discussed sites that they like and sites they don't. You may have even looked at them together and discussed the pros and cons of the design, navigation, special features, etc. Although *your* site certainly doesn't need to resemble anyone else's, I've found that it often helps to have a basic understanding of the common generic forms, which is the purpose of this chapter.

If several weeks have passed since the team's initial meetings, it might be a good idea to take a second look at your favorite sites as you discuss the issues presented here. Also, if your web team hasn't yet brought in a designer, now is a good time to do so since any decisions made at this point will have a major effect on your site's visual appearance.

7.1 Generic types

With few exceptions, websites fall into one of two generic types:

- Functional
- Topical

There are also two *techniques* that should be mentioned as these are often grouped with the true generic types and have a direct bearing on the site structure:

- Multi-target
- Associative

Even though the designer has yet to draw a single sketch, the choice of generic type will invariably dictate the way users get around the site, which automatically brings us back to the role of the information architect. That's because menu labels, site organization, and the number of individual links a visitor is exposed to will change tremendously from one type to another. Of course information can also be arranged alphabetically, such as telephone listings, or chronologically, such as back issues of magazines, or geographically, such as lists of sales outlets, but these techniques are usually used deeper into the site and virtually never form the main site structure. That's because these organizational devices are only effective when people *know* exactly what they're looking for. The structures for Wireless Application Protocol (WAP) applications, which allow dynamic data access from mobile phones, are somewhat different from traditional website structures for this precise reason. Since most WAP users *are* looking for specific information, simple alphabetical indexes can be used on the top levels with great success. You'll find a more detailed discussion of WAP in Chapter 19.

Functional sites

The main menu of a functional website typically consists of *verbs* that describe *actions* the visitor can take (an example is shown in Figure 7.1). For example, "buy" and "lease" represent functional choices that might be made by people looking for an expensive piece of equipment, a car, a pho- tocopier, etc. There's often a friendly, interactive feel to functional sites.

Functional sites are often used by (but not limited to) companies that provide a particular service rather than a physical product. The func- tional style, however, suggests that a company is able to define enough specific tasks to make the site work efficiently without feeling forced. For example, a site featuring a function labeled "Meet the family" to describe the basic corporate organization is forced. The same functional label, when used in a more literal fashion on a personal website may work just fine. Web browsers (and by extension many corporate intranets and

Figure 7.1

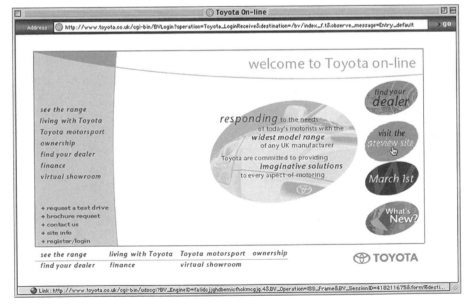

The UK site for Toyota features a good range of functional menu choices.

extranets) are usually highly functional in character since they are basically task-oriented applications.

A functional site can also be very effective on sites where there isn't all that much content to present. In these cases, the user experience is often defined by some online feature, which naturally lends itself to functional labels.

Topical sites

Without question, the vast majority of websites are topical (subject-oriented) since it's an easily recognized convention used in virtually all other reference materials, from encyclopedias to the Yellow Pages. Menu items are usually *nouns* that describe specific *things* a visitor can investigate (see Figure 7.2). For practical reasons, most sites are limited to about

Figure 7.2

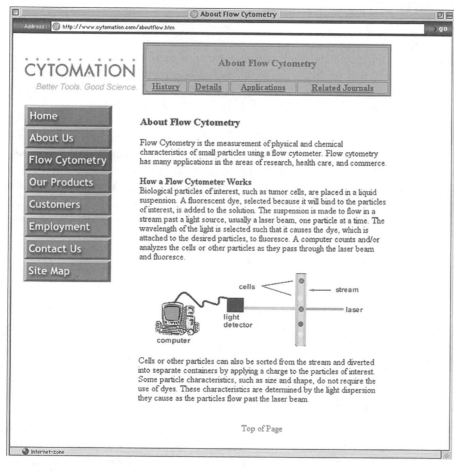

A fairly typical "topical" site.

ten major topical divisions (see Chapter 8). As such, the topics displayed on a homepage must be chosen with great care since they define (and limit) the range of information visitors can reasonably expect to find. Naturally, the choice of topics and labels will usually be determined by the needs and expectations of the primary audience. Although we're getting a little ahead of ourselves, here's an example of how an audience dictates topics.

If you were putting together a site that sells food, you might arrive at the following chunks of information:

- meat

- vegetables

- fruit

- fresh

- canned

- frozen

All of these words are topical and might make good menu labels. However, the first three will probably be most useful to supermarket customers and the last three better suited to a wholesale site aimed at supermarkets. For the sake of comparison, a functional site would use words like "buy," "prepare," and "eat." In fact, most topical sites also include some functional options, of which "search" is probably the most common.

One of the dangers of topical sites is that they can become terribly impersonal: for some reason these sites seem to inspire writing in the third person. This is, of course, easily avoided if you're aware of the problem.

7.2 Generic techniques

The next two sections discuss *techniques* rather than generic *types*. Each brings with it a number of potential problems that you may encounter if you choose to use one of them. Ways to work around these problems, or to avoid them entirely, come later in the book. The techniques are described here merely to give you a better idea of your options at this point.

Multi-target sites

This is a technique that enables visitors from different target groups to access editorial content specially created to meet their group's needs (as shown in Figure 7.3). A typical example would be to divide a site for household paint into a special area for professional painters/contractors and

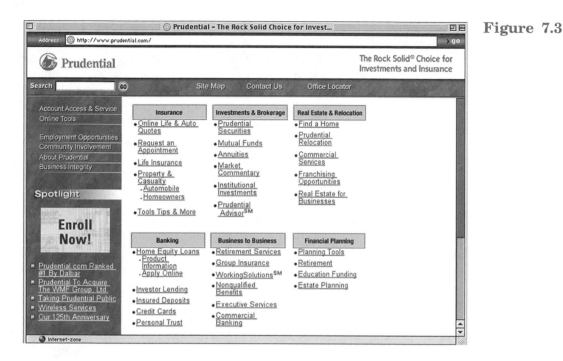

Figure 7.3

Prudential Insurance has divided their main site into six subsites, each with its own particular target audience.

another section for homeowners. Chapter 16 is devoted to some of the more specific techniques involved in the creation of multi-target sites and the development of one-to-one relationships. For now, here are some of the highlights.

One of the first matters the web team (or the site owner) needs to decide is whether or not to let the various audiences see each other's information. Pharmaceutical companies, for example, are not keen on patients looking at information provided for physicians, so access to a particular area will often require some sort of registration along with assignment of a pass-word – a so-called "closed" site. In some instances, a real person reviews the registration information and decides whether or not to let a visitor in. Also, sites that demand subscription fees will typically practice strict visitor segregation, giving users a peek at what's available, but not the whole site. Don't think these are strictly for adult sites, more and more reputable online magazines are adopting similar revenue-generating tactics.

If the site is "open" and visitors can choose from one of several profiles, the information architect faces several problems. The first is that visitors may cut themselves off from something elsewhere on the site that might interest them, but doesn't fit neatly into their chosen profile. Alternatively, the architect doesn't want to get into a situation where the same information is endlessly duplicated, thus defeating the whole purpose of a multi-target site. Finally, if editorial content is to remain truly target-specific, site maintenance can become a real nightmare.

Bear in mind that many visitors, are worried that they will miss out on something by joining a particular profile. Some actually click through several profiles just to make sure they get it all. If you've duplicated lots of basic information, these visitors may think your well-intentioned profiling was just a cheap trick to make the site look more sophisticated and end up with a very negative impression.

Associative sites

Also inaccurately dubbed "metaphor" sites, associative sites use a technique that draws on an organizational or functional analogy to create a particular look and feel: sometimes cute, often confusing. The most typical examples are those that supply a graphical representation of an office reception area on which visitors can click doors leading to the marketing department, sales department, or whatever. One of the dangers of this technique is that visitors may expect functions that you cannot or will not provide (clicking on the receptionist, for example, never leads to the search

Figure 7.4

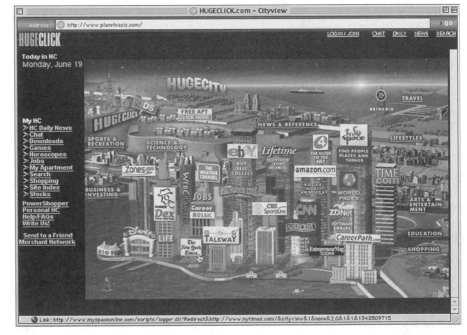

The PlanetOasis.com portal/community provides visitors with an elaborate cityscape to explore, plus more detailed "blocks" of buildings on the lower levels that group related links. Like most associative sites, the elaborate design is really nothing more than a fancy way to display buttons.

page, which would represent a genuine metaphor in this context). At any rate, associative sites are usually just a fancy way to display buttons, which may be all you want to do (Figure 7.4).

A department store might try to recreate the individual floor plans. A supermarket might recreate the produce department and the delicatessen section in stunning 3-D. The possibilities are endless – and extremely limiting. Like functional sites, associative sites can also become forced if you insist on pursuing an analogy to the bitter end. They can cause terrible confusion, too; think back to all those times you've had to ask a clerk where something was in your local supermarket! If you build a site up around your office, and people have never *been* to your office, visitors will invariably have trouble finding their way around.

Now that I've said all these nasty things about associative sites, it could be this is just the thing you're looking for! Swedish-based Electrolux, a leading manufacturer of household appliances, has used this technique to surprisingly good advantage. Take a look at their Electrolux home at www.electrolux.com (Figure 7.5). It's a first-rate solution. Even the forced analogies work well thanks to the quirky cartoon characters who guide you around. Another good associative site is "Mama's Cucina" created by the makers of Ragu Spaghetti Sauce, which you'll find at www.ragu.com.

One of the good things about associative sites is that they seem to encourage browsing; many professional information architects use the word "serendipity." In other words, visitors may be more likely to accidentally

Figure 7.5

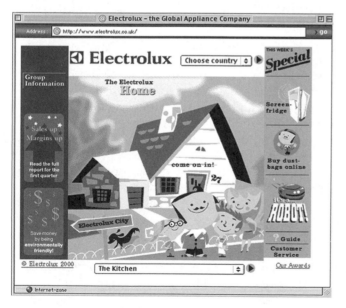

The Swedish home-appliance giant, Electrolux, first launched this wonderfully entertaining associative site back in the mid-'90s. The design remains optimized for older browsers and smaller screens.

come across something that interests them that they would have missed if they had simply drilled down through a topical hierarchy.

A brief word about metaphors   "Metaphor" is without question the most misused word in the current web lexicon and I hope people will eventually adopt more appropriate terms. To set things straight, a computer's "memory" is a verbal metaphor. Using a "lightbulb" to symbolize an idea is a widely recognized visual metaphor. However, using a graphic icon depicting a shopping cart to represent an electronic product-gathering system relates far too directly to the actual function to be considered a true metaphor. It is a simple analogy. Remember, although all metaphors are symbolic, not all symbols are necessarily metaphors!

The English language has many words for analogies, functional and otherwise. There are precious few words that are synonymous with metaphor so please, let's not redefine it.

7.3 Generic styles

Not so many years ago, experts talked about first, second, and third generation websites, referring primarily to the use of graphics. Now, with faster computers, higher transfer speeds, and better development tools, these "generational" distinctions seem less important. In the meantime, several generic *styles* seem to have evolved, each with its own target group in mind.

Newsletter sites

Used extensively by service providers specializing in content delivery, including CNN and Microsoft, these sites have adopted a "front page" style that includes as many individual links as possible, generally arranged in three columns. On the left, visitors find the primary navigation; a wide center column contains the main editorial content. Contextual links and/or local navigation are frequently arranged to the right.

Often, the main content area features a news story or two describing recent events. In general, it would seem that the broader the spectrum of potential users, and the bigger the range of information to be provided, the greater the need to provide an extensive opening menu so users can quickly locate their particular area of interest. Many portals (Yahoo, Excite, etc.) build on a similar theme, although the main content area is devoted to a hierarchical index of external sites rather than a news story.

One of the more interesting newsletter sites is www.britannica.com (see Figure 7.6), which has been designed in dynamic modules so that visitors are exposed to new featured topics on a regular basis. If you visit the site several times over the course of a week or month, you'll see how things change. This clever concept, which turns a very static product like the

Figure 7.6

The innovative Encyclopaedia Britannica site builds on dynamic modules, and features syndicated content from the Washington Post.

Encyclopaedia Britannica into a very dynamic site that also integrates syndicated content from other sources, was pioneered by Razorfish (www.razorfish.com) in New York. Razorfish also developed an easy-to-use set of design templates to help the Britannica editors manage the site and maintain its dynamic character.

Image sites

These feature a lot of white space, animated graphics and other attention-getters in the main content area. Many design groups favor this format, which forces the user to move the cursor arrow around to various objects or words to see if it turns into a hand (as shown in Figure 7.7), thus indicating an explorable link. I call this "mouseploration." Although lovely to

Figure 7.7

A typical image site from the German automobile giant, Audi. Each of the four animated images in the main content area functions as a link.

look at, these sites can be very tedious to navigate. Most users prefer to see all of their menu choices at the same time, particularly since menus are often so ambiguous. However, if people don't have (or don't need) a clear idea as to where they want to start, image sites can be very entertaining. The most effective image sites are those that limit the use of this technique primarily to the opening page.

Tile sites

Tile sites often have main pages that consist of many different visual elements (usually without any text) each functioning as a link to another section in what some architects have termed the "hypertext model." Here, each page is linked to one or two other pages, which in turn are linked to one or two others in a big, confusing knot. The hypertext model is actually one of the oldest interactive models, and formed the basic structure for the first computer adventure game, Advent, conceived by Will Crowther back in 1972 (Figure 7.8).

Even if some kind of hierarchy exists in a site of this type, the concept quickly falls apart as users reach deeper levels since the navigational technique is so terribly limiting. However, this style is often favored by graphic artists when advertising their own work (Figure 7.9) and, more often than

Figure 7.8

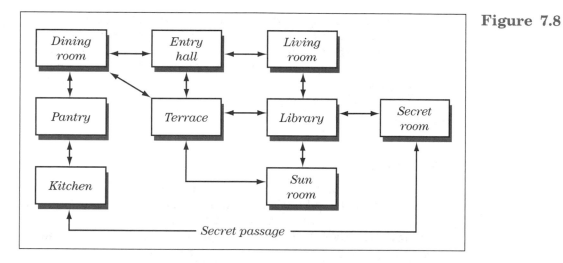

A hypertext structural model as used in an adventure game. The technique is not particularly well-suited to websites.

Figure 7.9

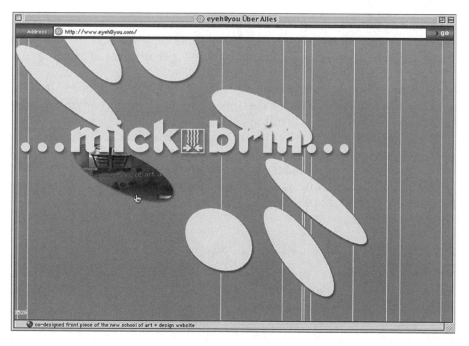

This typical tile site features nine clickable areas, none of which are labeled. All in all, it took me over 15 clicks to find the e-mail address!

not, each picture on the main page only has a single subpage. By forcing a lot of mouseploration, these sites create the impression of being larger and more sophisticated than they actually are. On the other hand, if the whole purpose of a site is to encourage random browsing and the visitor has not come to find specific information, the technique can be fairly effective. I call these tile sites because each click is like whacking a ceramic tile with a hammer to see what's behind it.

Traditional sites

You've probably seen a million of these, which feature a header of some kind, a navigation bar at the left, a content section at the right, and may also include a dynamic "billboard" containing the latest news. Although I call this style traditional, it does not necessarily mean dull. It merely implies that elements are placed more or less where people have come to expect them to be. It's like putting a table of contents at the start of a magazine; and in this respect both *National Geographic* and *Wired* can be considered traditional. This no-nonsense style seems to be one of the more effective from a business-to-business standpoint.

Search sites

These sites feature a minimum of hierarchical navigation. Instead, they rely on a search engine to provide a list of links that will lead the visitor to (hopefully) the appropriate function, topic, or specific piece of information. This style is very effective when users know what they're looking for and know how to search (alas, most people don't). The genre is not restricted to AltaVista and HotBot type sites, but is also used extensively by companies or service providers who offer so many individual choices that it is difficult to provide effective traditional navigation. In this respect, eBay auctions (www.ebay.com) is basically a search site, even though traditional navigation is available to those with the patience to use it. Bibliofind (www.bibliofind.com), an Amazon subsidiary specializing in used books, is a particularly effective search site.

Hobby sites

This group represents the garbage bag of web design. There are no rules and the architecture can be simply atrocious. The worst sites force you to click through the site in a linear fashion ("Click here for next page"). Others have far more navigation than content, and often lots of under construction warnings. Not long ago, hobby sites demonstrated significant design and navigational innovation, although the really good sites were few and far between. Today, most of the truly interesting ideas have been developed by professionals. Granted, I'm wrong in calling this a generic type, but I did think they needed to be mentioned.

Evolution on the web

Generic models are certainly not the *only* styles around, but they're among the most popular these days so it helps to become familiar with them. In the years to come, new styles will evolve as more sophisticated web conventions are established. For the time being, though, very few navigational devices can be taken for granted. That's why the good sites have a tendency to resemble each other: visitors stand a better chance of recognizing and understanding navigation and structure if they've already seen it somewhere else. That's also why traffic signals are red/yellow/green from Toledo to Tashkent.

Here's an interesting piece of trivia: I heard recently that over 100 years passed from the time Gutenberg invented printing using movable metal type until someone got the bright idea to add page numbers. Happily, web evolution seems to be moving somewhat faster.

On a related note ...

If you've been reading this book in a linear fashion, the time has come to start working on an actual structure, which is described in the next chapter.

In the meantime, I'm reminded of a story told by the composer Richard Rodgers (of Rodgers and Hammerstein fame) in his autobiography. His partner, Oscar Hammerstein, frequently wrote the lyrics to a song *before* Rodgers had composed the melody. Rodgers noted, however, that Hammerstein always hummed while he wrote and asked why. Hammerstein replied, "It's easier to put words to music – any music – than writing straight poetry." He never let Rodgers know *which* tunes he had used as a rhythmic framework so that Rodgers' own work was not influenced.

In other words, although it may help if you have one of the generic styles in mind when you start arranging your information, don't let the *site* style cramp *your* style. They're listed here merely as a source of inspiration.

Keep in mind ...

- This section has more to do with design than architecture, but it's important background for you to have.

- Most sites are either topical or functional. These are generic *types*.

- Don't force your site into a functional form that it doesn't really fit.

- Multi-target and associative sites represent specific *techniques*.

- Examining the generic *styles* can provide inspiration for your team.

- The more you take advantage of established web conventions, the easier you will make things for your visitors.

Before you go on

At this point, I'm going to assume that *you* are the information architect and have the blessings of your team. On the other hand, if you are *not* the architect, here's what you need to know if you want to make life easier for someone who is.

I'm also going to assume you have been involved in several lengthy meetings during which the basic goals were defined, the primary target audience was identified, and the informational requirements of the site have been determined. Moreover, you probably have some particular style in mind for the site, although this is not an absolute necessity. Finally, you may have some ideas as to special features you'd like to include and have cleared these thoughts with a programmer. So far so good.

Putting together the first structure

At long last, the time has come to start arranging the information in some logical fashion. This is usually *not* a group effort – at least not a very large group since so many minor decisions need to be made along the way. If an eagerly democratic team insists on discussing each and every detail to death, the project will probably never get off the ground. Remember, this is merely the *first* structure and will be discussed and edited by the team at a later date, so it's not as if no one has anything more to say.

8.1 What you want to accomplish

Essentially, a structure is an organizational diagram of your site, consisting of individually labeled boxes connected by lines (as shown in Figure 8.1). Each box represents a page and each line represents a link. Many site maps look like this and for good reason: they're showing you the structure of the site! What we're trying to do now is to take all the chunks of information we've created, arrange them in a logical hierarchical fashion, and give our boxes easily understood names or *labels*.

As mentioned in Chapter 6, there are also hypertext-driven sites and those built up around a database function. However, 99 percent of the time, a site will be based on a specific hierarchy, which is what we're going to work on now. I might add that unless you understand the basic problems and advantages of a hierarchical site, it's virtually impossible to build other types of sites successfully.

8.2 What are you going to put on the first page?

CNN uses their main page to present the day's top news story. Apple Computer advertises its latest model. CBC tells people who they are.

And "What is CBC?" you're probably asking. Well, it's an advertising agency in Copenhagen that I once worked for. You know what CNN *is*. You know what Apple *does*. But if you don't enjoy this kind of market recognition (few do), you'd better tell (or show) people right from the start who you are and what you do (Figure 8.2).

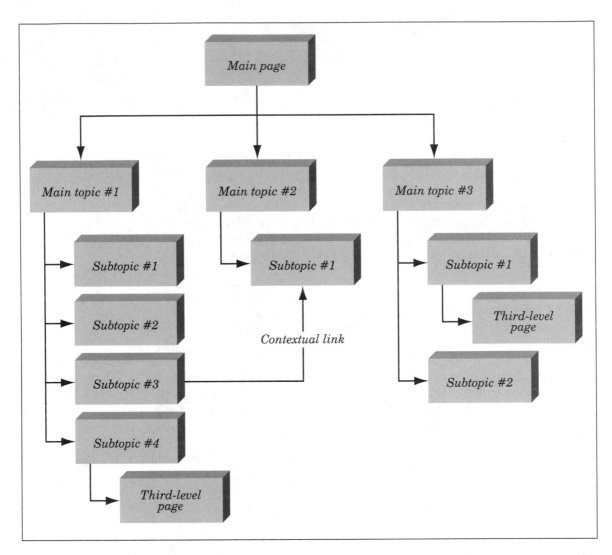

Figure 8.1 *This is the type of informational "blueprint" you're out to create for your site: a sensible arrangement of all the individual chunks of information, plus an indication of their internal relationships. Not very exciting to look at perhaps, but without one your site may not turn out to be very exciting to use either.*

Some sites get so wrapped up in announcing their company's latest achievements, they forget that visitors may not know who they are. In short, whatever you do, make sure you put important information like this right there on the first page so people can see it. Don't force them to click on "About the company." If your phone number and address are important, then don't hide them under "Contact." This is what's known as "surfacing" information: bringing frequently needed information to high (or higher) levels within a hierarchy. Finally, when the time comes to *design*

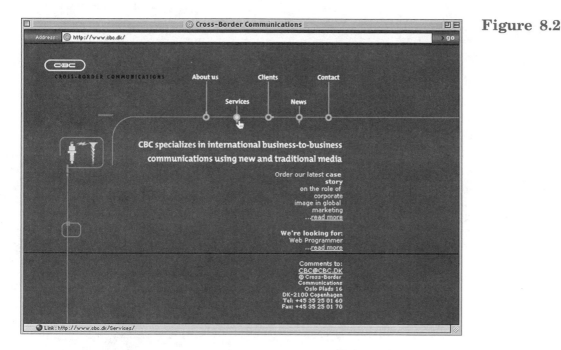

Figure 8.2

Short, sweet, and to the point. Visitors don't have to dig around, or even scroll, to discover what CBC does or where they're located.

the page, make sure all of this information is immediately visible, without forcing visitors to scroll down. Newspaper editors call this "above the fold" – which means putting headlines and important news on the portion of a folded newspaper that's visible when it's stacked at the newsstand (see Figure 8.3).

By the way, the actual text content on the first page is also important since some search engines don't register keywords and other coded "tags" (metadata) but actually "read" what's on the page. As such, content providers should be prepared to write an introduction that includes the most important words and phrases so your site is properly indexed by the search engines that come to look you over.

Now that that's out of the way, let's get down to business.

8.3 Getting started

To begin with, look through your chunks of information, and see if any natural divisions are starting to form. If your information is written down on separate pieces of paper, try sorting these into logical groups: for example, general background information, technological information, product/service information, contact information, etc. However, since

Figure 8.3

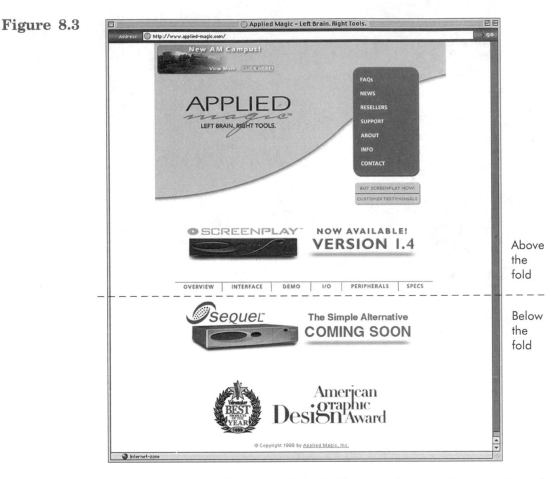

Above the fold

Below the fold

Visitors using a small screen will probably overlook the information located below the fold on this homepage, in this case a new product announcement and a prestigious industry award.

these are basic generic categories, I don't expect your structure to necessarily follow this model. Choose what's right for *your company*, not someone else's.

There is no right or wrong way to do this. In fact, some teams ask the individual members to do their own sorting and then compare the categories they come up with afterwards. I have to confess, I've used this method myself and have rarely learned anything new, but it does have value if you need to activate the other members of the team.

Of course, if you're completely new to all this, the team approach may help you along. It's also useful if some team members disagree as to how topics or functions should be divided (wall paint = use, latex = property). This is a good time to talk through the problem in detail. You may recall from the discussion of chunking in Chapter 3 that we retained all the various sets of possible subgroups for future reference. Now's the time to look through them again and attempt to reach some kind of decision.

Another source of structural information is the table of contents in any existing product catalog. This probably won't be an enormous help, but it's worth taking a look anyway.

Our immediate objective is to define the basic site divisions so people who don't necessarily know what they're looking for (or what you can provide) can quickly gain an overview of the site content. These will be your main menu choices.

8.4 Menu length: the myth of "seven, plus or minus two"

Back in 1956, George A. Miller published an article in *The Psychological Review* entitled "The Magical Number Seven, Plus or Minus Two: Some Limits on Our Capacity for Processing Information". It has since become *the* classic study relating to our ability to receive, process, and remember information. If you want to read the whole article, you'll find loads of links on the internet if you search for "plus or minus two."

Many experts cite this work, explaining that people are best able to differentiate between about seven different things, plus or minus two. Hence, they conclude that an "ideal" menu should have between five and nine items.

In actual fact, there is little in this excellent piece of research to support this conclusion with regard to menus. The number "seven, plus or minus two" merely refers to what we can retain in our short-term memory. And we're not necessarily asking our site visitors to *memorize* our menus. Dr. Miller himself points out that we are all perfectly capable of differentiating between any of several thousand words. Moreover, if the seven, plus or minus two rule was truly valid in terms of websites, then why should it only apply to the main menu? For reasons I've never understood, the lower levels are never subjected to the same standards.

So what's the proper number of menu items?

The actual number of menu items you can reasonably use at any given point in the navigational process depends entirely on what your visitor *knows* at that particular time. In other words, if you've landed on a page explaining that your friend Kate has candles based on holiday and seasonal themes, 20 menu choices leading to turkeys, pumpkins, etc. probably won't bother you. Just think, nobody gets very worried when a page in their address book has more than nine names – even if they aren't in alphabetical order. That's because we *know* who the people in our address books are.

However, if Kate had listed all of her candles on the first page, visitors might become overwhelmed and/or confused, particularly on their first visit. We can quickly scan a list of related items, but when different categories of information are presented, we like to see these items *grouped* accordingly. An address book usually features alphabetical groupings, which work well for most people since they know what they've called people – "Andersen, William," "Uncle Bill," etc. Which brings us back to our main menu.

A good rule of thumb is, the less people know about something (your company, for example) the more general the menus have to be. This is also the reason so many web page generators produce fairly good sites based on generic categories: five to ten main site divisions are pretty much the norm, but not because of seven, plus or minus two. The truth is, the more choices you provide, the greater the chances you will have to get more specific than you really want to on the very first page. There may also be design-related issues that will limit the number of divisions, but as the information architect, don't let the designer reduce the usability of your site for purely aesthetic reasons.

Above all else, you want to make things *easy* for your visitor. Twenty main menu items may force visitors with more than one informational need to do a lot of clicking back and forth between subpages and the main menu. Also, there may simply not be enough information to justify a separate category that has been established merely for the sake of completeness. This is often where the amateurs get into trouble and end up posting under construction signs.

Of course, newsletter-style sites can have 60 or 70 links on the opening page, sometimes even more. If you examine these sites, though, you'll find that most of the information has been grouped in a far smaller number of physical areas on the screen, each with its own clear and concise label.

Figure 8.4

Here are some possible menu items for a site designed to promote Kate's handmade candles. Even though there are only nine items, the list is difficult to scan because of the haphazard organization and frequent switching between topical and functional labels. You can read more about this in Chapter 10.

Dipped candles
Molded candles
Beekeeping
Organic colors
Holiday delights
Make someone smile
About Kate
Ordering
Patriotic themes

Dipped candles
Molded candles
Holiday themes
Patriotic themes
Humorous themes
About our bees
About our organic colors
About Kate
Place and order

Figure 8.5

With some minor editing and better organization, the new list is much easier to read, although these choices will probably need to be revised as the lower levels begin to take form.

8.5 Sets of menu items and completeness

Perhaps this is the right time to talk a bit more about the concept of "completeness." Let's say you're an online computer dealer and your basic product divisions are:

- Computers (CPUs)

- Screens

- Printers

- Scanners

- Modems

- Cables and accessories

Granted, there are other ways to cut this cake – small businesses, home office, etc. – but that's not the point right now. What *is* important is that all of these different sections are critical to someone who wants to put together a computer system. However, where's the section on CD-ROM reader/writers, external drives, etc.? These items don't fit neatly into the above categories, although one would be tempted to click on "Cables and accessories" in the hope that they're hidden there.

It's fair to assume that anyone in the computer business who's supplying all of these other components will also sell disk drives and CD-ROM readers/writers. If this category was temporarily left out because the section was too expensive or difficult to implement (do I see an "Under construction" sign on the horizon?), the site is going to be disappointing to users. In other words, as far as possible, the *whole* package needs to be presented if the site is to succeed.

Figure 8.6

In principle, websites should always be under construction, but there's rarely a reason to advertise the fact! Most visitors interpret these signs to mean "launched and forgotten" – and never return.

It's a question of "Don't bite off more than you can chew." As the information architect, when these situations arise, which they constantly do, you need to find out if there's a reasonable way around the problem. Usually the solution is to eliminate other parts of the site that are less "mission critical." Retaining your unique selling proposition, though, *is* mission critical since visitors may not feel like revisiting a fairly run-of-the-mill site, thus missing out on all the marvelous improvements you make a few months later.

In the example above, one could make a good case for leaving out scanners if this would make it possible to present storage media instead. That's because you can get a computer to work without a scanner, but storage is usually a much more integral part of the system. In any event, make sure your voice is heard when the final decisions are made.

At the other extreme, some companies already have an existing multimedia production on diskette or CD that they want to put on their website. However, if extensive information exists for one product line, but next to nothing for any of the others, visitors will often note this imbalance and wonder if these other products are even worth considering. After all, the site owner doesn't seem to think much of them.

8.6 Developing homogeneous systems

As I have already mentioned, people generally find it easier to scan a list of related items. In terms of defining menus, the idea is to create identifiable *systems* in which the language structure and subject of the labels are consistent (see Figure 8.7). This, too, improves comprehension.

For example, take a look at this menu for a site designed to sell roof tiles, featuring targeted information for three different audiences:

- Homeowners

- Contractors

- Architects

Let's say that the company also provides specialized design services that help people calculate how many tiles they will require for a particular job. Since this service is relevant for all three target audiences, it's

Figure 8.7

Banana
Oranges
Apple sauce
Exotic fruit
Citrus fruit
Canned
Cider

This is no joke! I actually found these choices on a super-market website: since when has "citrus fruit" not included "oranges"? Note that the site owner couldn't even decide whether to make things singular or plural!

tempting to use the following menu:

- Homeowners

- Contractors

- Architects

- Design services

However, our menu now lacks consistency since three of the options represent people and one option represents a product/service. A homeowner looking for professional guidance will be left in doubt as to whether to click on "Homeowners" or "Design services" since both options are appealing.

Even though the design services are important and the site owner may want to surface this information, it would probably be better to highlight this topic *under* each of the target categories so that visitors are properly channeled without having to make a judgment call.

An example of main page and menu considerations

Probably over half the total time you spend on the structure will be used defining the initial choices you give visitors when they come to your site. You might even consider writing a short mission statement for each of your main sections that defines its specific purpose within the overall context of the site. Not only will these help you clarify your thoughts and avoid ambiguity, they often provide an important indication of how your detailed information should be sorted. If your main menu items are worked out carefully, you'll generally find that the other pieces of information fit surprisingly well into the overall scheme. If they don't, you need to find out *why*.

Just for fun, let's say we're working on our friend's handmade candle site and we've decided to use part of our opening page to provide a basic introduction to the company and its products. It might read as follows:

> Kate's Candles specializes in high-quality candles made from beeswax harvested from our own beehives. Many of our candles are hand-decorated using natural, non-toxic organic colors.

Having set the scene, and reviewed our information chunks, we've come up with the following menu items:

- About Kate
- The candlemaking process
- Our products
- How to order
- Links

Suddenly we find that we have information about Kate's beehives and organic colors that don't seem to fit very well under "The candlemaking process." So, we add a new category about "Raw materials," which we soon change to "Wax and colors" because the other title didn't sound friendly enough. Besides, we've already established in the introduction that there is something special about our wax and colors and don't really want to talk about anything else. (Kate buys cheap wicks at her local hobby shop.)

We also discover that when visitors click on "Our products" they're almost immediately forced to choose between molded or dipped candles. Can we divide this menu into two items right from the start? Well, maybe we *can*, if we tinker a bit with our introduction.

> Kate's Candles makes and sells high-quality candles made from beeswax harvested from our own beehives. Our molded candles come in both square and round designs, plus a range of special decorative shapes and figures. Our dipped candles feature the typical finely tapered shape that has come to represent quality and elegance in a mass-produced world. Many of our candles are hand-decorated using natural, non-toxic, organic colors.

At this point, you're probably wondering if the information architect has to write everything, too. The answer is no, but the example does show why the architect has to have a pretty good idea of what information needs to be included by the content provider in order to make the site work. In this case, it's necessary to acknowledge the fact that before a visitor can click on a menu labeled "Dipped candles," they have to know the difference between these and "Molded candles." The revised introduction helps educate the visitor, although it's far too wordy.

8.7 Wide and narrow?

It's a well-documented fact that users looking for specific information can scan through a list of menu options faster than they can navigate through a hierarchy. Obviously, if you've divided your own address book into "men" and "women," it will take longer to find a particular name than if you have used alphabetical categories.

When visitors know what they're looking for, long lists of menu choices can be perfectly acceptable. However, you need to remember that the more detailed the label, the harder it will be to scan. If your long list includes things like "XJ-120-M mega pixel digital zoom camera," visitors are going to have a tough time scanning through it. And if the next item on the list is an "XJ-140-S mega pixel digital zoom camera," you'd also better make sure visitors know the difference between these models.

8.8 Good structures are invisible

Most visitors need to be able to establish a quick "lay of the land" when they arrive on your main page. They like to look around, read your menus, and get a basic idea of what they can expect to find. That said, there's no indication that visitors ever establish a mental model of your deeper structure – although they do catch on to hierarchies. In fact, for most people, the site's structure remains more or less invisible until it ceases to meet their needs; just think, you rarely discover that your umbrella is missing until it starts to rain. But back to the lay of the land.

One step at a time

A university, for example, may choose to start out with a long list of the individual departments. The problem is, visitors might want information regarding registration and tuition. So, in most cases, the information architect will categorize the site so the opening page requires at least one menu click before plunging into more nitty-gritty details. As mentioned before, long lists are fine if the information they contain is homogeneous in character. In other words, you can mix apples and oranges, as long as people are reading a list of fruits.

In general, the less people know about your company, organization, products, or services, the greater your need for a narrower and deeper hierarchy. But "deep" doesn't necessarily mean eight clicks. In actual practice, by the time a visitor has clicked two or three times, a good structure will usually have landed them squarely on the information they're seeking. If you have key pages that are four or five clicks off your main menu, you should probably think about revising things. This is a suggestion, not a hard and fast rule – there will be exceptions on most sites.

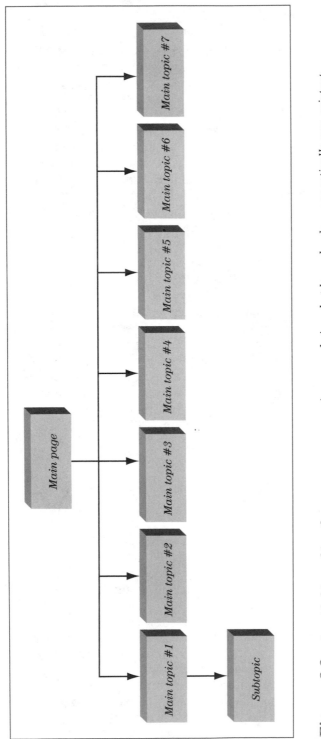

Figure 8.8   *In wide hierarchies, there are numerous main menu choices, but lower levels are practically non-existent.*

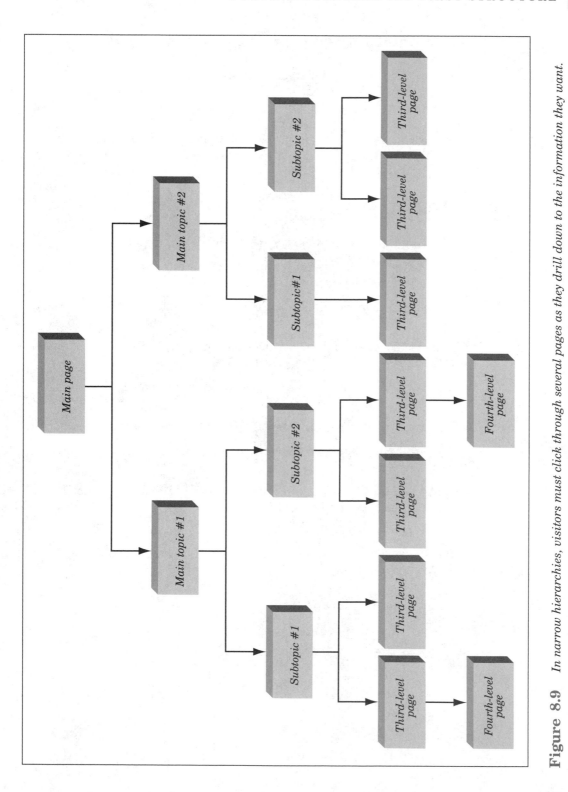

Figure 8.9   *In narrow hierarchies, visitors must click through several pages as they drill down to the information they want.*

8.9 Structuring from the bottom up

Having spent so much time talking about creating a hierarchy from the top down, it's worth noting that you can also work the process in reverse. In other words, you figure out what you want your visitors to *do* on your site (order a product, for example) and then work backwards to determine the overall categories. You may find that your upper levels will change to clarify and/or simplify the process by surfacing key information or functions.

Keep in mind ...

- Creating the first rough structure is usually not a group effort.

- Make sure that visitors can immediately see important information, such as your address, on the first page.

- Your basic menu divisions should let visitors quickly gain an overview of your site.

- There is no golden rule about the number of menu items you can have. But ...

- Too few main menu choices will probably create too narrow a hierarchy.

- Too many main menu choices will probably force you to be too specific.

- The less people know about your company, the more general your menus will have to be.

- Don't bite off more than you can chew! Make sure all the "mission critical" parts are in place.

- Keep your menus homogeneous in character.

- Ideally, by about the third click, a visitor should have found what he or she is looking for.

Getting it down on paper

We're not finished with our initial structure, not by a long shot. However, it might be helpful at this point to discuss some of the practical aspects of getting your ideas down on paper. If you already have a system that works well, just give this chapter a quick skim and go on to Chapter 10.

All of the following "scripting" techniques have their good and bad points. I've had great success with both Post-its and ordinary written outlines – as have many of the people with whom I've worked. The other methods described here are included for the sake of completeness. Choose whichever method suits your personal style best, but don't get so bogged down in the mechanics of transferring your ideas to paper that you lose your train of thought!

9.1 Post-its – again

Back in Chapter 4, I recommended writing down the informational labels on Post-its. They are even more useful when the time comes to *arrange* the information and are considerably faster to work with than, say, file cards pinned to a bulletin board. Usually, I stick the main menu items in a horizontal line across the top of a big piece of paper or cardboard (or even a roll of brown wrapping paper) and then place the lower level information in vertical columns under the appropriate heading. Often, I use different colored Post-its to represent different types of functions, for example, yellow for static screens, blue for dynamic screens, and green for pop-ups and other special features that aren't really screens in themselves.

I also stagger the Post-its to indicate that certain pages are subordinate to others, so-called "subpages." Figure 9.1 shows a simple schematic representation.

You probably won't want to draw in the individual links at this point. First of all, you'll undoubtedly rearrange things a dozen times before you are satisfied and the links will just get in the way. Second, in most cases, you'll simply *know* where most of the links are supposed to go. If, however, some link is not particularly obvious, for example a link to a page located somewhere else, then write a Post-it with the link information, "Link to XYZ" or something similar and add it as though it was an ordinary subordinate page. Finally, you'll probably want to give your visitors several

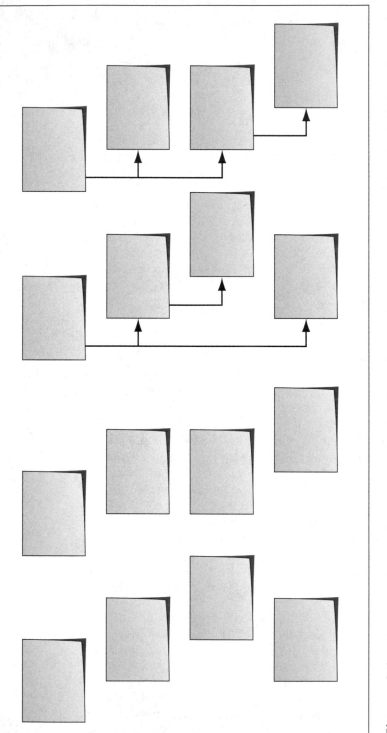

Figure 9.1 *Arranging Post-its, shown with and without links. In most cases, you won't want to draw in the links until you are finished moving things around.*

different navigational options, drilling down through your hierarchy is merely one of them. For now, we just want to give everything a logical "place to live" – no matter how it will be contextually linked to other pages later on.

9.2 Written outlines

A surprising amount can be accomplished using an ordinary word-processor. The technique is identical to the way some of us were taught to take notes when we were at school. Figure 9.2 shows a simple example. Please note the numbering system, which will prove very useful later. Actually, you'll probably want to wait to add the numbers until you're through swapping information around so you don't have to waste time constantly renumbering your outline.

The problem with written outlines is that many people find them difficult to understand. As such, if you choose to do your first rough structure as an outline, make sure you turn it into a diagram before you present it to anyone. This will invariably save you a lot of explanation later on.

If you were going to draw this same structure as a diagram, it would probably look something like Figure 9.3.

Figure 9.2

1.0	**Products (main menu = 0.0)**	
1.1	Red products	
	1.1.1	Rose
		1.1.1.1 Technical specifications
	1.1.2	Carmine
		1.1.2.1 Technical specifications
		Hyperlink Reference story (5.3.3)
	1.1.3	Vermillion
		1.1.3.1 Technical specifications
1.2	Blue products	
	1.2.1	Sky
		1.2.1.1 Technical specifications
	1.2.2	Cornflower
		1.2.2.1 Technical specifications
		1.2.2.2 Customer testimonial
	1.2.3	Navy
		1.2.3.1 Technical specifications

A typical written outline done on a word-processor.

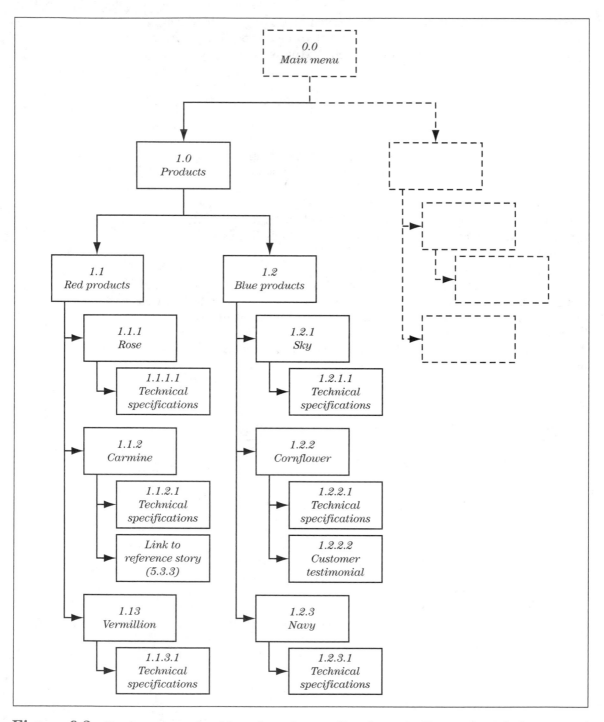

Figure 9.3 *Here's an example of how the written outline shown in Figure 9.2 might be expressed graphically.*

9.3 Mindmapping

Mindmapping (as illustrated in Figure 9.4) is an interesting notational technique that was developed to help people remember things better, organize their information, understand relational links between two subjects, etc. Entire courses in mindmapping are now taught at colleges and universities. Personally, I'm not convinced this is the best way to start a structure, but since so many so-called "creative thinking" programs are based on this technique (including a lot of website generators) I feel I ought to mention it.

When you mindmap, you start with a blank piece of paper and several colored pens. Draw a small circle in the center and label it "Home." Each time a new subject comes up, take one of the pens and draw a line out from

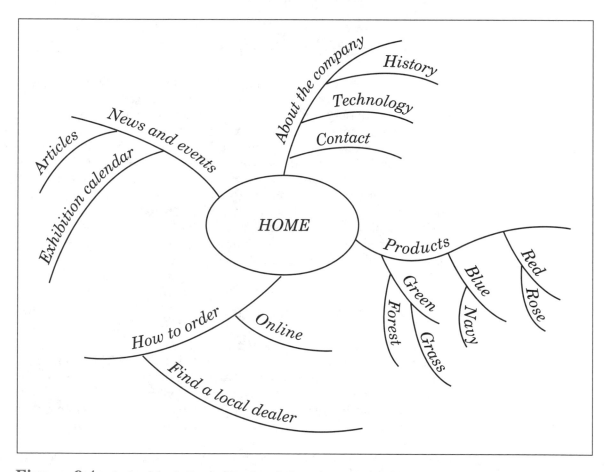

Figure 9.4 *A simple mindmap. I've found the technique useful for note-taking at an early stage or preliminary conceptual diagrams, but it's a bit confining when the time comes to put together a detailed structure.*

the circle using a new color for each subject. Give each branch an appropriate name. When a topic relates to one of these main subject branches, draw a smaller branch out from the main branch and label it accordingly. The colors help you visualize information that is related, plus any links you need to add from one branch to another.

Since mindmapping was basically developed for note-taking, it assumes that the person doing the mapping is listening to a lecture or presentation of some sort. As such, the main divisions have usually been defined by the person doing the talking. The problem here is, we need to define these main branches *ourselves*.

If you're already familiar with the technique, you might find it useful if the sheer mass of information you have gathered has you overwhelmed. I've found it most useful during very early discussions and for taking notes during the information-chunking stage.

9.4 Electronic applications

Although there are many special programs designed to help you create a structure, in reality, they merely help you *draw* a structure – they won't help you make the key decisions. If you need to make a nice copy of your structure for presentation purposes and your word-processor doesn't have this feature, then feel free to go out and buy a special application – Visio from Microsoft is something of an industry standard for PC users (www.visio.com); Inspiration (www.inspiration.com) is the best product I've found for use in mixed Mac and PC environments.

Just remember, the ability of these tools to increase your creativity is questionable at best – you think with your mind, not a machine! Actually, I've long suspected that the mechanics of learning and using these programs actually *hinders* the creative process.

9.5 Numbering systems

At one stage or another, you're going to have to give each and every page on your site a unique reference number (Figure 9.5). This eliminates any doubt as to which page an architect, content provider, designer, or programmer is referring to during the production phase.

The written outline shown in Figure 9.2 uses a numbering system that has become more or less standard among multimedia professionals. Here's how it works.

Normally, the main page (the first true content page your visitors encounter) is numbered 0.0. All the main menu subjects are numbered 1.0, 2.0, 3.0 and so on. Subpages to a particular main menu subject are numbered 1.1, 1.2, 1.3 (or 2.1, 2.2 as appropriate). Subpages to these

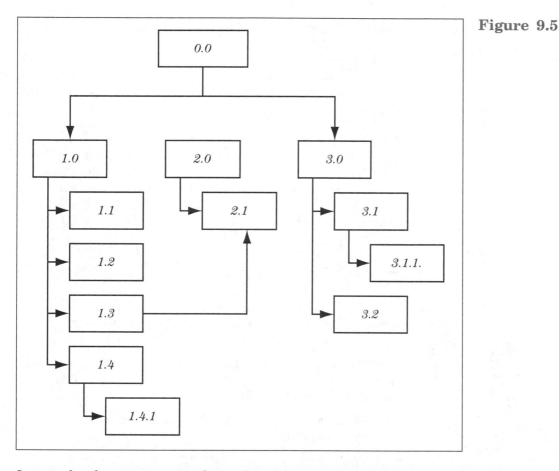

Figure 9.5

In a numbered structure system, the number of digits (excluding 0) tells you how many clicks you are from your opening page.

"second-level" subjects are numbered 1.1.1, 1.1.2 and so on. If your site is split up into subsites, or is physically located on several different servers, it is sometimes useful to give the numbering system a prefix such as M for main, or P for press lounge, or whatever.

This system may appear terribly pedantic, but it's also terribly effective. There are two other advantages to this system as opposed to simply numbering everything from 1 to 100. First, the number of digits (excluding 0) always tells you how many clicks your visitor has had to make to reach a particular level. Second, the number of digits also gives the content provider an immediate indication of the level of informational detail required on a particular page. More about this in Chapter 11.

Remember, during the early stages, you probably won't want to waste time filling in a numbering system because of the constant changes you'll be making.

9.6 Making notes about specific content

Occasionally, the information architect will want to jot down a specific editorial requirement for a particular page. For example, when we examined the introduction to the "Kate's Candles" site, we discovered a need to differentiate between molded and dipped products.

When I work on a structure, I often keep a notebook in which I jot down specific content details I don't want to forget. I mark the individual page label on the outline or diagram with an asterisk, or a circled letter, or some other code that refers back to my written notes. Later on, when the time comes to start gathering the editorial content, I transfer these notes to the special numbered form created to guide the content provider and production staff. You'll find a sample in the appendix.

Keep in mind ...

- Post-its are ideal for arranging and rearranging information during the early structural phase. It helps to use different colors to represent different types of screen functions.

- Ordinary written outlines typed on a word-processor can also be used for organizing the basic structure, although they don't provide as many visual clues as a physical diagram.

- Mindmapping is more useful for note-taking, although some information architects use the technique for basic structuring.

- Electronic applications make things look nice, but don't expect them to enhance your creativity.

- Don't number all the pages from 1 to 100 (or whatever). Rather, use a hierarchical numbering system such as 1.0, 1.1, 1.1.1, etc. The number of digits (excluding 0) tells you the number of clicks it took to reach a particular page.

Calling things by their right name

10

What you actually call individual menu items on your site depends on what you want your visitors to get out of your efforts. If you choose to be cryptic, there'd better be a good reason. In most cases, ambiguous menu labels are a prime source of irritation for visitors – so take the time needed to get them right. Although this chapter dwells on something that most professional information architects find incredibly obvious (particularly those with knowledge of cataloging and indexing techniques) most other people have never given the matter much thought, which is why I'm bringing the subject up now. Feel free to skip this chapter if you already have experience in this area.

10.1 Speak your audience's language

I don't think there's an organization in the world that hasn't invented its own internal language. For example, one company I know numbered each room of their new office complex before they moved in so the movers knew where to put things. The stockroom was assigned the number "20" and to this day, people still say, "I'm going down to 20 to get some envelopes," – including staff who only recently joined the company. One linguist I know calls this "secret-society language."

As a rule, companies absolutely *adore* their secret languages, which can make things very difficult for those of us who aren't members of the club. For example, what may be a "protective coating system" to business insiders is merely "paint" to the rest of the world. (In fact, I recently heard about a group of beekeepers who insisted on being called "apiculturalists" – which is as absurd as it is accurate.) In short, menu items, particularly on the first few levels, need to have labels that people immediately understand. As you get deeper into the site and have defined more and more of your terms, the menus will sometimes change in character. But avoid taking too much for granted since visitors are easy to confuse. Also, no matter what you do on the lower levels, make sure your primary navigation doesn't change: this will foul things up tremendously!

Be consistent

Remember, you want to create *systems* of labels that are consistent in both language and content so that they don't confuse your visitors. Moreover, once you introduce and define a term, stick to it! For example, if you've established that you have "molded candles," be careful not to confound things by suddenly referring to them as "poured candles."

10.2 IA SNAFUs

One of the most common problems is the use of acronyms. Of course, if an acronym is widely accepted shorthand, such as "CD" for "compact disc," you won't run into many problems using this as part of your label. However, if one of your products is an "Interactive Network Adaptor" that you routinely shorten to "INA," you'll probably have to define the acronym several times (possibly on every page on which it appears) and only use it as a label on pages where it *is* defined. Unfortunately there are no hard and fast rules about this. You'll have to take a look at the problem as it occurs and let common sense be your guide. In general, though, if a subpage can be accessed from only *one* other page, you probably won't need to redefine your abbreviations, for example on a page of technical specifications that can only be accessed from the page displaying the detailed product description. The link for the subpage can therefore be labeled with the relevant acronym without causing any major confusion.*

10.3 **Eliminating doubt**

A good rule of thumb is: any menu item that makes a visitor backtrack because they've made the wrong choice is badly labeled. Although this is hard to test accurately during the initial structure phase, it's worth checking your structure through "role-playing" to see if you're meeting the needs of your various target audiences effectively (see Section 4.3).

Let's assume at this point that your menu labels are sufficiently descriptive and visitors know what you mean by all your terms – and you've sorted out the differences between "global" and "international." The next thing you need to watch out for is if visitors can possibly be in doubt as to which of two menus will bring them to a specific piece of information. Here's an example.

If you sell orchestra instruments, you might have the following menus:

• Strings

• Brass

---

* And in case you're wondering, a SNAFU stands for "situation normal – all fouled up."

- Woodwinds

- Percussion

We'll assume that the rest of the site makes it clear that "strings" refers to violins, cellos, double-basses, etc. and not guitars. However, someone looking for a saxophone may be in doubt since it is made of brass but uses a reed like a woodwind. Now if we assume the visitor *knows* something about musical instruments, they'll probably look under woodwinds, since this is usually how saxophones are classified in orchestral terms. However, is it fair to assume that visitors understand traditional orchestral terms?

If each of these menus also displays submenus listing the individual instrument types, there's no problem. Unfortunately, this is a design/ content decision that will have to be made *now*, which is not always practical. So, we need to make a judgment call: we either leave things as they are, or investigate alternative menu labels. Here's a revised set:

- Strings

- Brass

- Reeds

- Percussion

These menu choices leave somewhat less room for doubt, although the label "Brass" might still cause confusion. At this point, though, we discover a *new* problem: what do we do with flute players? Normally, they're considered woodwinds, but aren't made of wood and don't use a reed. Do information architects need to understand content? You bet they do!

10.4 Improving the scent

In information architecture terms, "scent" refers to the hints a visitor gets from the words and types of words used to label particular subjects. In the above example, we keep running into problems because we cannot be sure that visitors are as well-versed in the vocabulary of an orchestra as we'd like them to be. So let's improve the scent by providing more explicit labels:

- Violins and other strings

- Trumpets and brass

- Flutes, woodwinds and other reeds

- Xylophones and percussion

Figure 10.1

Since rollovers and pop-up screens may contain special content, I sometimes represent these in the structural diagram as individually named and numbered boxes in parallel with the actual menu choices. The 0 in the number tells me that this isn't really a new screen.

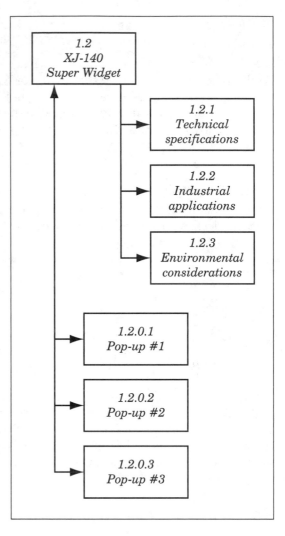

This is usually the point at which the designer throws his or her first tantrum. After all, these labels don't fit nicely into graphic buttons! It's probably also the time to suggest the alternative listing with submenus mentioned earlier:

Strings:
    Violins
    Violas
    Cellos
    Double-basses

The designer may suggest a drop-down menu to consolidate the visual appearance of the page. Unfortunately, your visitors will not be able to see all the options at once, which will slow the navigational process. However, it may be the only acceptable compromise. The latest browsers include a variety of new features that allow you to create rollover informational screens. These automatically appear when your cursor rolls over a particular area without the need for special browser plug-ins or other extra software. In other words, when a visitor moves the cursor to a particular menu item, a list of subsidiary menus can be made to automatically drop down (Figure 10.1), either to improve the scent or provide further navigational options.

At any rate, you'll invariably run into other problems related to limited space as you try to define your menu labels, if not here, then on deeper levels. Whatever you do, don't just take the easy way out – whatever that may be. Spend a little time to consider (and reconsider) different alternatives before you finalize your labels.

10.5 Cute labels

As a professional writer, it's terribly tempting to justify one's own existence by coming up with snappy (read = cute) functional labels instead of cut-and-dried topical ones. Unless you are working on a site with a decidedly functional thrust, these sorts of labels can cause a lot of problems for users and thus decrease the usability of the site.

For example, if Kate's Candles had a menu item labeled "Make someone smile," the label is going to need a lot of textual or graphic support if people are to fully understand what she means. Is she about to present us with a range of humorous candles? Does she want us to send someone a gift? Perhaps she also sells novelty wax teeth! The point is, if there is a reason for injecting cute labels, do so (perhaps you want to encourage random browsing). Just make sure the ends justify the means – usually a loss of comprehension on the part of the site visitor.

10.6 The graphic designer's (i)con game

Back in 1996, screen icons were all the rage, mainly because they pepped up those dull first-generation websites that consisted of long, gray columns of text. Within months, menus no longer had words, they had little pictures. Unfortunately, a picture is not always worth a thousand words. Try creating an icon for "storage media" or "molded candles." The chances are, only the designer will recognize the true meaning, first-time visitors don't stand a chance.

Here's an interesting icon I just came across. It's a picture of a light switch. There was no further explanation (unless you were clever enough to read the target URL that appeared in the browser's status line when the

Figure 10.2

These icons rely on the accompanying labels for comprehension. Their main function is to distinguish site tools from the main navigation, located just above.

cursor turned into a hand). The icon in question was on a Danish site, and in the Danish language a light switch is called a "kontakt" – which can also mean getting in touch with someone. In other words, the light switch was a cute Danish pun leading to a page of contact addresses. However, people *have to know the real meaning* in order to get the joke – which makes it useless as an icon!

Successful standalone icons are invariably those that refer to generic navigational functions like home, e-mail, back, and forward. Virtually all other icons require descriptive text of some sort, no matter how clever or self-explanatory we may think they are. As always, the menu description must be both accurate and informative – *this* is what should dictate the length of the menu item, *not* the physical size of the button. Any description that starts to become the least bit cryptic should be rethought.

In short, icons can provide valuable visual support for written labels (Figure 10.2), but don't expect them to rescue one that is poorly defined or missing entirely!

You can't brainstorm labels

I'm sorry to say, but writing labels isn't something that can be effectively accomplished in a group, you're going to have to work out most of them on your own or with a professional writer. If you *do* throw things up for discussion, you'll invariably waste a lot of time bringing the others up to speed, explaining the pros and cons of the various alternatives – time that could have been better spent on other aspects of the project. If you don't believe me, try it yourself. Far better to present a complete, edited list and explain why you did what you did before inviting comments.

Keep in mind ...

- Avoid secret languages. Speak your audience's language!

- Beware of acronyms that may confuse your visitors.

- If labels aren't immediately understandable, find out if there is something else you can do to improve their "scent."

- Cute labels often create unnecessary confusion as to their true meaning. Use them sparingly.

- Icons can rarely stand alone. Nor can you count on them to rescue a poorly chosen label.

- Defining precise labels at this stage isn't usually a group effort.

11   Structuring the lower levels

Quite frankly, what you do now is going to make or break your site. Although I said earlier that if your main menu was structured correctly, all the other bits and pieces would probably fall neatly into place, this *doesn't* happen automatically. Not only do you have to give a little thought to arranging your chunks, you also need to determine the proper degree of informational detail in each click along the way. But one thing at a time …

11.1 The pros and cons of shell structures

For practical reasons, many large sites are structured and designed by professional consultants who are not necessarily content providers. These outsiders supply the basic "shell" and let the site owner plug in the editorial content. Since shell structures have received a lot of bad press from the usability experts, I thought I'd take a moment to discuss them.

One of the popular definitions of a shell site is one in which about half the underlying content can be removed without necessitating changes in the main menu. The implication is that shell sites are far too general and therefore don't work very well, which is simply not true.

If we take a moment to think about a *real* menu in a restaurant, we'll probably see it divided along the following lines:

- Appetizers
- Main courses
- Side dishes
- Desserts
- Beverages

This is the basic shell. Happily, it's easy to understand, so when the chef decides to add something new, there's generally little doubt about where it should go. Millions of restaurants use this shell and most customers have no trouble ordering a meal, so it's fair to assume that the system works.

The problems often attributed to shell sites, actually apply to *all* sites: if content at lower levels is not labeled correctly, or is not properly linked to other related pages, the hierarchy gets too deep and people get lost.

Remember, a shell is merely a single part of a site – like fenders on a car. Shells are not the site itself! The lesson to be learned is this: *navigation and content are two inseparable issues*, which means someone with a good grasp of information architecture (and the site's goals, target audience, and content) should be consulted each time new pages are added. Without this ongoing expert input, even the best sites can soon become a confusing mess.

11.2 Ensuring you have editorial content on each page

Sounds pretty obvious, doesn't it? Well, let's take a look at the following structure for the subjects accessible from a typical "About the company" menu:

1.0 About the company
    1.1 Mission
    1.2 History
    1.3 Organization
    1.4 Research and development
    1.5 Quality control
    1.6 Sales and service
    1.7 Worldwide addresses

Although it looks reasonable at first glance, there's one major problem: what are you going to tell your visitors on page 1.0? If you had designed this structure yourself, you might have decided that 1.0 was going to contain a summary that touched on all of the subjects covered on the subpages. On the other hand, you might find that you have nothing much left to say on the subpages since you put it all in the summary to begin with; the mission page will probably be particularly repetitive. This is often the case when there's only enough information for a short paragraph about each of the issues – usually bits chopped out of the printed corporate brochure (although your content providers should really be rewriting for the web).

A good information architect will weigh the pros and cons and probably do one of the following:

- move "Mission" up to 1.0

or

- suggest a short article touching on each of the subjects on a single page or

- suggest a short introduction with a list of hyperlinked bookmarks leading to relevant information further down the same page.

What makes this discussion important, is that your programmer needs to know if there will be one page or eight pages – and your structure must indicate this. Moreover, your content provider needs to know how to tackle the task of writing. If a page basically functions as a menu for lower-level topics, make sure these topics really deserve a page of their own before you force visitors to click down to a deeper level – or force a content provider to create a lot of unnecessary verbiage.

11.3 Levels of detail

Most communications experts agree that information can usually be presented with three levels of detail. A journalist, writing a news article might define these as:

- headline
- lead
- full story

Now you may be thinking that everything you need to say should be presented in three levels, but this isn't the case. Sometimes you'll have important background material that clarifies issues brought up in the "full story" – a fourth level of contextual links. In other instances, you might be able to tell the whole story on one page. The point is, if you need to use two or three pages (often to home in on one particular product or subject) make sure you've got new and useful information to give your visitors each and every click along the way.

Good journalists try to include answers to Who, What, When, Where, Why, and How in their lead. This helps newspaper readers skim the start of an article to decide if it contains something of interest to them. Here's a typical example:

> At a press conference in Washington yesterday, the President announced that due to a drastic rise in road fatalities, proceeds from a special tax on automobiles will be used to finance highway safety improvements nationwide.

Who = the President

What = announced special tax on automobiles

When = yesterday

Where = in Washington

Why = reduce road fatalities

How = finance highway safety improvements

In many respects, a good summary on a website (for a product, service, etc.) will try to accomplish the same thing. Salespeople use the term "elevator speech" – what they would say to a potential customer if they only had a 30-second elevator ride during which to pitch their product.

In web terms, the three levels of information are often as follows:

- Label
- Short summary
- Detailed presentation

and possibly

- Supporting evidence (contextual links)

Here's a structural example of how these might apply to a specific product and its related pages.

1.0 Products (general label)

    1.1 Green products (specific label and short product summaries)

        1.1.1 The XJ-140 Super Widget (detailed description)

            1.1.1.1 Technical data (supporting evidence)

In this example, the content for page 1.1 must contain short product summaries or other relevant information to explain the difference between the XJ-140 and the XJ-120 (or whatever). Often, each short description is accompanied by a separate hyperlink leading directly to the more detailed description. At any rate, by the time the visitor has reached the actual product description on page 1.1.1, they're expecting (and entitled to) a full, detailed presentation.

Remember too that if you're presenting a product, you want to create a shared reference. If you cut the information up into too many small pieces, it may be difficult for the visitor to form a unified impression.

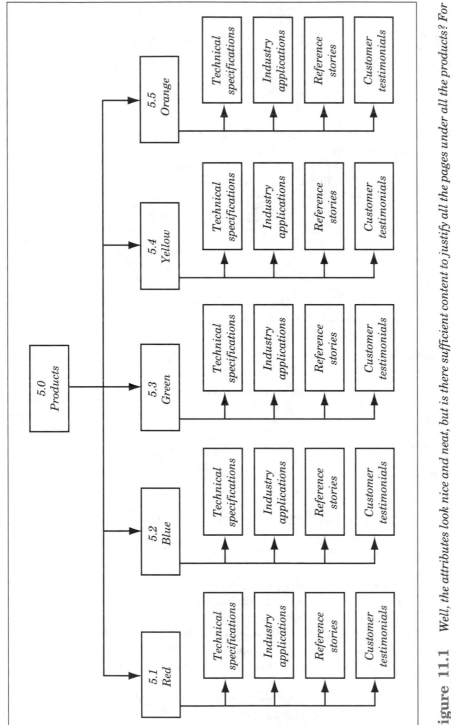

Figure 11.1   *Well, the attributes look nice and neat, but is there sufficient content to justify all the pages under all the products? For example, if the "Orange" products are a recent addition to the range, it may be tough to find customer testimonials.*

Visitors should be able to anticipate levels of detail

As far as possible, try to attain a similar degree of detail for all of the items contained in a particular menu. If one choice brings visitors to a long informative page and another choice in the same menu provides nothing more than a verbose rehash of what they already know, you've got a problem. Most visitors have no objection to using a few clicks to get somewhere if the informational rewards make it all worthwhile. Returning visitors may be mildly irritated, but only if your hierarchy is absurdly narrow or your graphics take ages to download. Also, please remember that these remarks apply mostly to people who are drilling down through your hierarchy; many will be bypassing the intro pages because they accessed a URL through a search engine.

Frequently during the structure phase, the information architect may think detailed information exists on a particular subject when in fact it doesn't (see Figure 11.1). This often occurs in the interest of "completeness" (see Section 8.5). If editorial content needs to be created, do so, but don't force a content provider to fill up a page with fluff just because it makes your structure look neat and organized.

11.4 Optimum editorial content length

Experts have studied this subject from every conceivable angle with no clear-cut answer in sight. Granted, you don't necessarily want to lead your visitors to a ten-page report after the first click, but after two or three clicks this may be perfectly acceptable. This is also the secret to avoiding exceedingly narrow hierarchies. If you're still holding elevator speeches after the third click, your visitors are going to get bored and leave.

Some expert at one time insisted that people like short text – about 5–10 lines. As a result, many sites are both short on text and short on content. In truth, the *right* length is really whatever you choose to make it, provided you aren't forcing your visitors to read through a lot of (to them) unimportant information before they get to what they really want. Web writing needs to be short and to the point, if for no other reason than the fact that people simply don't like to read from their computer screen (and read about 25 percent slower, too). However, if a visitor has asked for a white paper from your company's technical archive, it's fair to assume this person really wants to read it. (The executive summary should have been on the previous page; the report itself should feature subheads and/or hyperlinked bookmarks.) Whatever you do, don't cut something up into tiny pieces (see Figure 11.2) or force visitors to perform a lot of back-and-forth navigation. Navigation designers call this phenomenon "pogo-sticking."

Figure 11.2

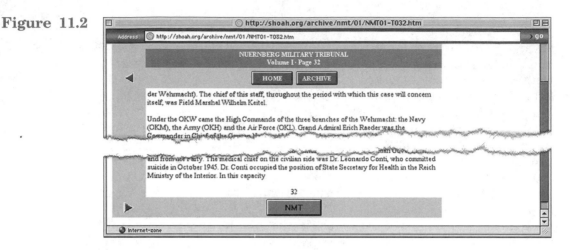

*This entire 900-plus page court document from the Nuremberg Tribunal can only be accessed one page at a time: a classic example of user-*unfriendly* architecture. Note that the page starts and ends in mid-sentence!*

Figure 11.3

Previous and next buttons are very convenient if visitors are going to want to browse through several related pages on the same informational level.

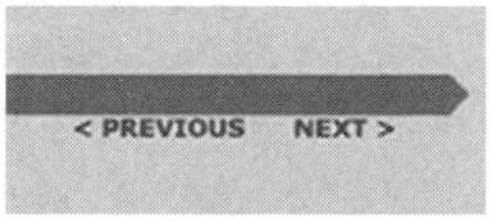

One final note

If you are certain that the same information is going to be needed by almost all visitors, make sure you don't bury these popular pages deep in the structure. If there doesn't seem to be any way to avoid this, you'll probably want to re-examine your main menu items, or at the very least, your second-level choices. In some cases, you may want to supplement the normal navigation with "Previous" and "Next" to avoid pogo-sticking (Figure 11.3), particularly if the visitor will want to browse through a large number of related pages. These will show up as specific links on your structure. On the other hand, avoid the "Click here for next page" syndrome in which visitors are forced to navigate through a large section in a strictly linear fashion *without the benefit of alternative hierarchical navigation.*

Keep in mind ...

- A "shell" structure isn't necessarily a bad thing, but it's only one isolated aspect of a site.
- Navigation and content are inseparable issues!
- You need editorial content for every page. Beware of pages that have been created merely as menus for lower levels.
- Don't force content providers to fill a page with narrative just because you think it makes your structure look neat and organized.
- Visitors should be able to anticipate levels of detail as they drill down through a hierarchy.
- Short copy is better than long copy – but if it takes more words to explain a particular subject, use them! Optimum length is dictated by the visitor's informational needs (and expectations) on any specific page.
- Don't force your visitors to "pogo-stick" between a menu and lower-level pages if they will probably want to read several related pages on the same level.

12 Getting the most out of hyperlinks

Thus far, we've mainly talked about the links leading to main subject areas. Usually, these are repeated on all of the other pages in one form or another and are separated from the ever-changing content, either because they have a different graphic design or are located in their own special "frame." Frames essentially break down the browser window into separate, smaller windows so you can scroll one area without affecting information in any of the others.

Now let's take a look at links that appear within the main content area and do not form part of the primary navigation. In case you skipped my definitions at the start of the book, a "link" generally refers to a graphic symbol or text of some kind that functions like a button to bring visitors to a new page. A "hyperlink" is essentially the same thing, but is usually set in the same typeface as the main content and is both blue in color and underlined: a well-established web convention.

Most of the following advice can first be put to good use during the design and production phases, and I don't mean to tread on the toes of other specialists. Nevertheless, the information architect needs to know what works and what doesn't work since the use of hyperlinks invariably has an impact on the final structure and the ongoing success of the site in terms of usability.

12.1 Contextual navigation

In Chapter 9, I mentioned that every piece of information had to "live somewhere," which is important if the basic hierarchy is going to work correctly. For example, I'll bet that your knives and forks "live" in the top drawer in your kitchen at home. However, "contextually," they are usually found next to the plates on the table when you sit down for a meal: you probably don't ask your dinner guests to rummage around to find them. In essence, this "rummaging" is what we want to avoid by providing convenient contextual navigation on our website.

Here's another example. In a traditional library, if there is only one copy of a particular book, the librarian needs to decide where it's going to be shelved. If you have, say, a collection of essays by Thomas Jefferson, where do you put it? Under political science? History? Agriculture? Architecture? American history? This is an important decision if the library is to be truly useful.

Happily, thanks to hypertext links, you can put the same information in several different places on a website simultaneously. What we want to do is to "surface" information according to the specific needs of a visitor at a specific time (see Figures 12.1 and 12.2). Let's say, for example, that our XJ-140 Super Widget is located in the hierarchy under the heading "Products." This is, after all, a natural place to put it. However, we might also have a special section for customer references, and down on the third level in the parallel hierarchy for "References", there's a mention of the XJ-140. It's reasonable to assume that someone reading this reference story might be interested in learning more about this particular product, so we create a special contextual link that leads the visitor directly to the XJ-140 page, thus eliminating the need for the visitor to drill down through the product hierarchy. In other words, we create added value for the visitor by bringing together related subjects, just like a wall represents greater value for a homeowner than a pile of individual bricks.

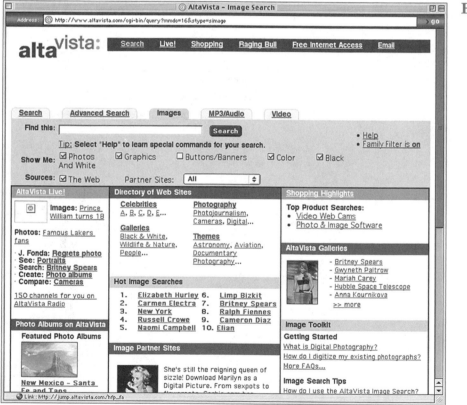

Figure 12.1

The AltaVista search page for "Images." Note the contextual links to a wide range of image sources.

Figure 12.2

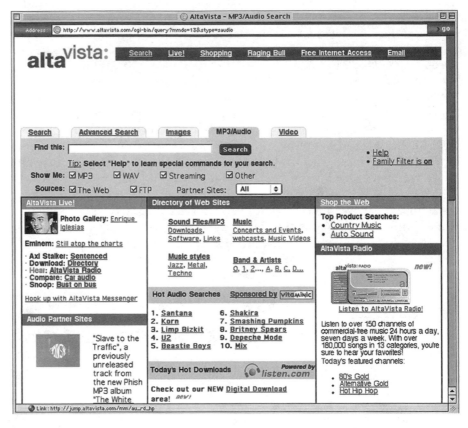

By clicking on the "MP3/Audio" search, all but the very top level links change to reveal useful contextual links to other music and sound sources.

I realize that this is a very short introduction to a fairly complicated subject, but if you understand the basic principle, you'll invariably find ways to implement useful contextual navigation on your own site (including links to locally relevant tasks as well as topics). You'll find more information on contextual navigation as it applies to audience-specific sites in Chapter 16. The rest of this chapter deals with some of the more specific hyperlink techniques and their associated problems.

12.2 Dynamic billboards

Let's go back to our candle site for a moment. It could be that Kate wants to use the main page to promote her seasonal candles. Or perhaps she's a very newsworthy woman and is regularly written up in various magazines. In this case, the architect might decide to turn the page into a dynamic billboard.

A dynamic billboard uses the main content area of the page (everything except the main navigational menus, etc.) to post news and other timely announcements (Figure 12.3). These separate stories are generally presented as a short synopsis which is hyperlinked to a page located somewhere else. For example:

Kate's Candles make the Fortune 500   The latest issue of Fortune now ranks the modest country candlemaker number 499 on its list of the world's largest business enterprises!

One of the rules of dynamic billboards (and all other hyperlinks for that matter) is that visitors are helped tremendously if your hyperlink is underlined and has a different color – I vote for blue. The fact is, people

Figure 12.3

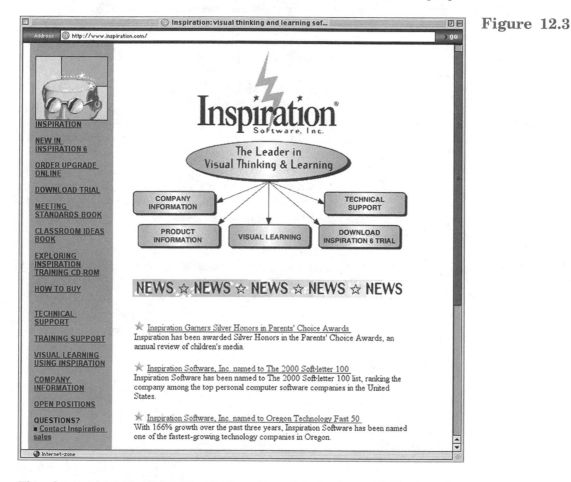

This dynamic billboard lets Inspiration (a major developer of diagramming software) surface key information about their company and products that would normally be relegated to a lower level in the overall hierarchy.

don't always *recognize* hyperlinks that look like part of your overall graphic design. I realize that this is a design issue, but since the technique is so important in terms of structure and usability, it's worth mentioning now. Links need to *visually* signal "LINK!". It's terribly unfair to expect people to shove their cursor arrow around in the hope that it will turn into a hand (mouseploration). Conversely, it's very misleading if you underline for <u>emphasis</u>, although I suspect no one under 30 does this much anymore!

Another alternative is to set your news story in any graphic style you want and then add "<u>Read more ...</u>" after the last sentence. Alternatively, you can tack on "<u>Full story</u>," another widely accepted form, particularly when referring to news articles.

The dynamic billboard technique is also useful on lower levels when you have to provide visitors with enough background information to enable them to choose between several similar (or similarly named) choices.

In fact, whenever you use hyperlinks, make sure you always give the visitor enough information to make an educated choice *before* they make their choice. I know I've said this before, but it bears repeating. Here's a little story.

A few years ago, I ran into the link "<u>Tiger Rag</u>" in the online edition of an in-flight magazine for a major airline. No other information was provided, although I could gather from the context that this was a feature article of some kind. Since I'm interested in ragtime music, I clicked – and was surprised to find a feature story about the golfer, Tiger Woods. Not only was the title of this article pretty silly to begin with, but without illustrations or other clues a visitor couldn't possibly know what the story was going to be about. If you want to be cryptic or mysterious (sometimes this is good), make sure your visitors will think it was all worthwhile when the page finally loads.

Last but not least, although dynamic billboards are terrific tools, you also have to be prepared to regularly update those that contain topical news, once a month at the very least. If your company doesn't have all that much to say, then a dynamic billboard may prove difficult to maintain. On the other hand, I get a dozen e-mailed newsletters each Monday from companies that clearly have no problem generating content, yet also have outdated billboards on their sites. The message here is: if you have a dynamic billboard, give it the priority it deserves.

12.3 Getting lost through hypertext

Since hypertext is such a useful tool, it's also subject to *misuse*. The first problem is when an individual description of some sort contains a large number of hypertext links embedded in the text. These links are usually terribly distracting and frequently cause readers to lose focus because the links make them curious and also force them to make a navigational decision: "Should I continue to read or jump somewhere else?" Moreover, instead of sending the visitor off on a logical path towards the information they really came for, these links may land people in some other section of the site where they'll get lost.

Let's take another look at the introduction to Kate's Candles, this time with a lot of hyperlinks:

> Kate's Candles makes and sells high-quality candles made from <u>beeswax harvested from our own beehives</u>. Our <u>molded candles</u> come in both <u>square</u> and <u>round</u> designs, plus a range of special <u>decorative shapes</u> and <u>figures</u>. Our <u>dipped candles</u> feature the typical finely tapered shape that has come to represent quality and elegance in a mass-produced world. Many of our candles are <u>hand-decorated</u> using <u>natural, non-toxic organic colors</u>.

I think you'll agree that this is rather more difficult to read. Besides, these links are not really saving the visitor many clicks since most of the same information can be accessed from the main menu. However, "decorative shapes," for example, leads to a lower level and visitors may become confused. I realize that there are various "You are here" types of navigational tricks to alleviate this problem, but these are only truly effective if visitors have learned to use them *before* they get lost.

Studies show that rather than pressing the back button on their browser, most visitors simply plunge ahead using the site's own navigation when they get lost. In fact, you can't even assume they'll think to return to the main menu to get out of their mess.

12.4 Visitors like hyperlinks

Several reports on user behavior indicate that website visitors *like* hypertext links, and often choose these before anything on the main menu. However, if there are no hyperlinks on the main page, visitors are forced to study the menu more closely. This is a good thing for the people who designed the site since they can control the visit and better predict levels of knowledge, although it isn't always a particularly user-friendly solution.

In general, I've discovered that hyperlinks located within the main content of the first page that lead directly to main menu topics work very well – and often have a higher click-through rate than other navigational options. These so-called "redundant" links take advantage of the visitor's natural sense of curiosity as long as you don't overdo it (as I did in the previous example). But be careful, if the label is radically different, people often get confused. In addition, main page hyperlinks that connect directly to pages on a *much* lower level can be very disorienting if they skip past important introductory information. Also, contextual links located on lower levels that lead directly to other low-level topics in another section can create problems for the visitor if the only method of returning to the previous page is by using his or her browser's back button. Now we're getting into the nitty-gritty of usability and navigation which is not the central purpose of this book, but as an information architect you're going to have to keep these problems in mind. Please take the time to read Jakob Nielsen's *Designing Web Usability* (Indianapolis, IN: New Riders, 2000): it's the best book yet on web design.

Orphaned subsites

Matters are complicated significantly if a link (of any kind) lands visitors on a separate subsite with no path back to the source. This is frequently the case when corporations have several different business divisions whose respective subsites are not linked back to the corporate site – so-called orphaned subsites. Companies with subsites devoted to individual brand-name products are often guilty of this oversight.

Avoid run-on hyperlinks

Although this is more a content issue, I thought I'd mention it anyway while we're on the subject. If you have to create a list of hyperlinked topics, people get confused if they see something like this:

Kate's Candles provides <u>molded</u>, <u>dipped</u>, <u>hand-painted</u>, and <u>decorative</u> candles of every kind ...

Visitors often overlook the fact that the space between the words isn't underlined and may perceive this as a single link. As far as possible, try to arrange your hyperlinks as columns if you have to present more than one:

Kate's Candles provides a wide range of high-quality candles for all occasions. Our range includes:

<u>Dipped candles</u>

<u>Molded candles</u>

<u>Hand-painted candles</u>

⋮   ⋮

These are actually poor menu choices, but I think you get the idea. In most cases, it's usually wiser to add longer, more informative hyperlinks (with better scent) at the *end* of a short paragraph:

[See how we harvest our wax](#)

[Visit our dipping shed](#)

[Read more about ...](#)

Short links

Visitors tend to overlook links when only a single, short word is hyperlinked. Enough said.

Orphaned links

In certain instances, a page can only be accessed via hyperlink from one other page. These pages are sometimes called orphaned links because they have no real home. A general site disclaimer is a good case in point; many companies choose to create a discreet link from the main page rather than include it in the general navigation. There's nothing wrong with orphaned links, as long as your visitors won't be placed in a position where there is an undue amount of pogo-sticking. However, if visitors must make a choice between several similar topics (or a direct product comparison), and each topic is described on its own orphaned link, you'd better rethink your navigation.

12.5 Splashes and other main page eyecatchers

We've all seen those spiky oval graphics on boxes of detergent and breakfast cereal announcing "New," "Improved," or "100 percent fat-free." In the advertising business, these are called "splashes," and they're just as useful on websites as they are on your favorite brand of cornflakes. In web terms, splashes are most often used to announce:

- free product trials
- competitions
- new features
- specially themed subsites (Press Lounge, Technical Forum, etc.)

Figure 12.4

Nilfisk-Advance is the world's leading manufacturer of industrial cleaning equipment. Special icons on their home page draw attention to key focus areas – particular sections that highlight the company's ability to solve specific cleaning problems.

In essence, splashes are merely flashy links to places you especially want your visitors to go – and with few exceptions, these pages should also be accessible from the normal navigation provided by the main menu (Figure 12.4). Splashes are most frequently located on the main page of a site. If you're running a competition, though, you may find it difficult to fit this feature into your regular structure, particularly if it is a unique occurrence (sometimes the related collection of pages for a special event is called a "microsite"). In this case, it may be more sensible to refrain from major structural changes to accommodate this temporary need and rely on a splash. You might also consider repeating the splash on other relevant pages deeper in the site.

About the only time you probably *won't* want to repeat a splash link in the main structure is when the visitor is an insider, such as a distributor or dealer who only needs to access your "Partner Zone" or some other closed, non-commercial subsite or extranet. On the other hand, it's doubtful you'll announce this feature in a splash to begin with.

12.6 Recommended reading

Now that I've (hopefully) got you thinking about some of the key navigational issues, you might be inspired to read more about the subject. Jennifer Fleming's book, *Web Navigation* (Sebastopol, CA: O'Reilly, 1998), is truly outstanding and ought to be required reading for all budding information architects. It's listed in the bibliography.

Keep in mind ...

- When it comes to hyperlinks, a good information architect knows what works and what doesn't.

- Contextual navigation creates added value for the visitor by bringing together related pieces of information.

- Dynamic billboards are wonderfully useful but require ongoing maintenance.
- Links need to visually signal "LINK!" if they are to be effective.

- When visitors reach an embedded hyperlink, they must make a decision: "Should I read on or go somewhere else?" If you keep asking them to make this kind of decision, they may miss the overall point of what you are trying to say.

- Redundant links take advantage of the visitor's natural sense of curiosity.

- Run-on hyperlinks may not be perceived as individual links. It's generally better to make a list of contextual links at the *end* of a paragraph or page.

- Splashes are tremendously useful for advertising special features of the site that you would like to highlight.

13 Adding secondary features

Almost every website will have several menu choices that are not really part of the main navigation, but are added simply to make things a little easier for visitors – site tools. Although some of these menu items may be important enough to include in the main menu, usually they are grouped separately. This lets visitors know that they are *not* subjects, but are more functional in nature. Here's a list of the most popular topics for these secondary menus:

- Home or Main Menu
- Contact (site owner)
- Feedback (webmaster)
- Site map
- Site index
- Disclaimer
- What's new
- About this site
- First-time visitors
- FAQ
- Quick links
- Search

Ideally, these links should be accessible from all the pages on the site and will therefore not have a major effect on the overall structure. However, this isn't always the case, so let's take a moment to discuss each of them.

13.1 Home (main menu)

Although most websites feature a company logo or some other graphic feature that functions as a link back to the main page, inexperienced users may not know about this convention. As such, a specific "Home" or "Main menu" link is extremely useful.

Actually, you do need to choose the exact label with some care, particularly if the homepage contains unique navigational links (a dynamic billboard, for example). Let me explain. In early 1999, I launched a hobby-oriented site that showcases a personal interest of mine, but which also allows me to test some of my pet theories without experimenting at my clients' expense. The homepage originally contained a large number of hyperlinked menu choices to keep the structure fairly flat and for about six months, I called this page "Home" in the main navigational bar. Using my site statistics (representing about 1000 user sessions per week) to track the main paths through the site, I suspected that visitors tended to forget that the homepage contained navigational choices that were only accessible from this single page. When I changed the primary navigation label to "Main menu" (my only change), visitors were soon spending more than *twice as much time* exploring the site. This just goes to show, menu labels *do* matter even for something as basic as defining the first page of the site.

13.2 Contact

Even when the basic contact information is on the main page, there should always be a menu option that brings visitors directly to a page containing the most important contact information: name, address, phone, fax, and e-mail. Of these, e-mail is probably the most important piece of information since *this* is usually what visitors are looking for.

In some cases the link will lead to a list of several main offices. In others, it may provide a list of contact names within the company itself. Sometimes, the page will have a different label entirely, such as "How to order." What you decide to include will depend to a large extent on your site's overall goal.

Although this is a content issue, when you provide an e-mail address, make sure that people *know* they're going to get a mail address. If you simply highlight a person's name, visitors may expect to get phone numbers and other information – or even a complete biography, particularly if they are reading a page outside the "Contact" area. As always, links have to be explained. Here's a typical example:

> Our board of directors includes <u>John Doe</u>, Managing Director, <u>James Doe</u>, Vice-president, Marketing, etc.

It would be better to add these links at the end of the page and leave no doubts in the visitor's mind:

> Our board of directors includes John Doe, Managing Director, James Doe, Vice-president, Marketing, etc.

Mail to John Doe: john@xyz.com

Mail to James Doe: jd@xyz.com

Other options include:

- For additional information, please contact info@xyz.com
- For additional information, please contact John Doe (john@xyz.com)

13.3 Feedback

"Feedback" generally means "Here's how you can tell our webmaster that something is amiss." However, this is still not a firmly established convention, which means that people may confuse the labels "Contact" and "Feedback." Moreover, if you have a site on which you present opinions of one kind or another, people may want to give feedback to the *site owner*. At any rate, make sure you include a direct e-mail link to whomever is in charge of site maintenance. A simple hyperlink "webmaster@xyz.com" is all that's needed, but represents a major convenience for those visitors who are willing to take the time to give you some free (and frequently valuable) advice.

13.4 Site maps

A site map is merely the site's structure shown in graphic or outline form with hyperlinked labels to all the individual pages (see Figure 13.1). Many users click on the site map automatically as though it were the table of contents in a book in order to gain an overview of the content. Other visitors resort to site maps if menu labels are ambiguous or the navigation is poor. Personally, I feel that if a site is well-structured, a special map is usually unnecessary, although if you don't have a search engine, the map provides useful global navigation. Whatever you decide, keep in mind that a site map is a *supplement* to existing hierarchical navigation. It shouldn't be an excuse for bad planning.

13.5 Site indexes

A simple, hyperlinked, alphabetical list of all the topics covered by a particular website can be tremendously useful to people who know what they are looking for and need a quick way to find a specific page. In fact, I

Figure 13.1

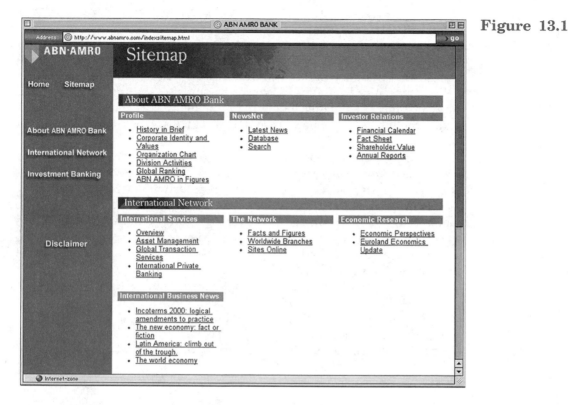

The site map for ABN-AMRO, a major Dutch investment bank, provides a convenient hyperlinked overview of the entire public-access site. A password-protected subsite provides stockmarket information and other special features designed to help investors monitor their portfolios.

personally feel that any site over about 25 pages that doesn't feature a search engine probably ought to have one. Remember, though, you need to constantly maintain your index as you expand and revise your site – many webmasters seem to forget this in the "heat of battle."

13.6 Disclaimers

Most sites have a disclaimer of some kind exonerating the site owner from responsibility for misuse of information contained on the site or to divorce the site owner from the opinions of those who may be using forums and chat rooms. Often, general copyright information is also included after the text of the disclaimer itself rather than posting a copyright notice on each individual page.

13.7 What's new

Normally, a "What's new" section is included as part of the main navigation when the information it contains is of general interest to visitors ("We just received the first deliveries of our new summer line" etc.). In many instances, a dynamic billboard on the main page performs this function, although, "What's new" is sometimes included as a secondary menu item.

One of the most important aspects of a well-maintained What's new section (no matter where it's located) is that it sends a strong signal to visitors that the site is truly dynamic and regularly updated. Far too many sites leave visitors with the feeling that once the site was launched, the company forgot all about it. On a related note, if individual pages are subject to regular revision (for example, lists of used books) it's helpful if you note the date of the latest page update somewhere in the editorial content, preferably at the top of the page.

An interesting variation on the What's new theme is the "Webmaster's diary"(see Figure 13.2). Here, visitors can find information about the more technical aspects of the site including news about reorganization, new sections, or mistakes that have been corrected. This is like a ship's log except that the entries are listed in reverse order so that the most recent note is at the top of the page.

Figure 13.2

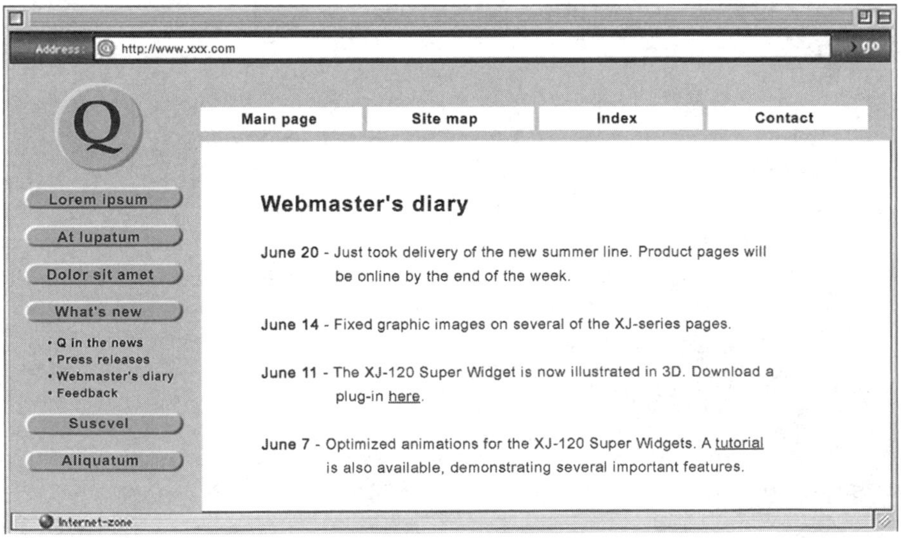

A typical webmaster's diary. This page sends a strong signal to visitors that the site is maintained and improved on a regular basis.

13.8 About this site

More and more, companies are combining their site map, webmaster e-mail address, disclaimer, and copyright information on a single page. Usually labeled "About this site," this combination page seems well on its way to becoming an established web convention.

13.9 First-time visitors

These pages are not always part of a secondary menu: they sometimes turn up in the main content area on the very first page, or may even represent part of the main navigation. Generally, these pages provide either technical information or guided tours.

Technical information includes information regarding special features or technical requirements for using the site. Normally, it shouldn't be necessary to send a visitor to a special page to communicate these things, but you might find a page like this helpful if you have a unique feature you'd like to promote. On the other hand, introductory guided site tours are far too frequently an indication that the architecture and/or the navigation is a mess, so visitors need some extra help.

In most cases, you'll probably be better off if you don't need a page like this!

13.10 Frequently asked questions (FAQs)

Usually called a "FAQ," this is merely a list of questions that many customers have had in the past (or could be expected to have), along with appropriate answers (Figure 13.3). These question-and-answer lists can be quite general, in which case they may appear in either the main or secondary navigation. Alternatively, if the FAQ list is very long or very detailed, it may be more sensible to divide it into several smaller documents, each placed in one or more relevant sections throughout the site.

In terms of information architecture, there really isn't that much more to say, apart from the fact that a FAQ provides an excellent opportunity to pull out a host of important details that visitors may otherwise overlook or have difficulty in finding. That said, a FAQ isn't meant to be a convenient miscellaneous section. Rather, it's your chance to collect a wide variety of related information from many parts of the site and present it in a specially structured document. If used correctly, a FAQ can also be a strong sales tool in its own right and can serve to lead visitors (via contextual hyperlinks) to appropriate goods and services.

One of the best-maintained FAQs I've seen, is on the United States Treasury Department's site (www.treas.gov/opc). It's a terrific source of

Figure 13.3

Two extensive FAQs on the Mondosoft site provide fast access to product and support information.

inspiration if you're unfamiliar with FAQs, and in this instance, it's practically a site unto itself and thus a very interesting structural solution.

13.11 Quick links

Quick links are simple drop-down menus, usually located on the homepage and sometimes on all pages, that provide immediate access to popular or frequently needed pages (Figure 13.4). In some instances, the entire hierarchy of a particular section of the site may be displayed. On many smaller sites, quick links are often used in lieu of a search engine; on larger sites, they usually function as a supplement to the existing navigation or lead to specific subsites.

Figure 13.4

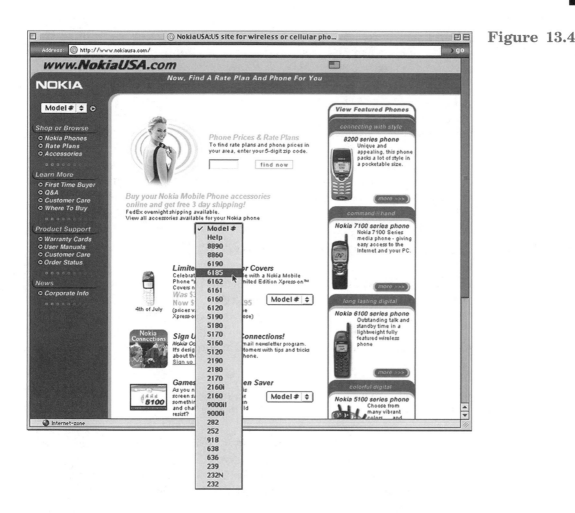

NokiaUSA rightly assumes that many visitors will be looking for information about specific phones. All of their many models can be immediately accessed via a convenient drop-down menu. (© 2000 NOKIA Mobile Phones, Inc. All rights reserved.)

13.12 Search

Jakob Nielsen, one of the world's foremost usability experts, has stated that if you have more than 100 individual pages, you should consider providing a search facility. This is not a bad rule of thumb, although more and more smaller sites also feature search engines to help people quickly find specific pages.

Like site maps, search engines are not the saving grace for badly structured sites, although at least one study indicates that about 30 percent of all website visitors head right to the search button rather than using the general navigation. I suspect this is because so many sites have been poorly organized in the past, many people simply got into the habit of *searching* instead of *navigating*.

Unfortunately, most visitors don't know how to use a search engine, and the problem is compounded by the fact that since so many different corporate search engines exist, visitors cannot be expected to learn how to use them all equally well. While we're on the subject of usability, an actual search field (where visitors can type in a query) as part of the general page design is generally preferable to sending people to a new page. Larger sites often provide both options – the dedicated search page is used to provide more sophisticated functionality.

13.13 Search engine options

If you have a database-generated site and are drawing on a controlled vocabulary (see Chapter 5), your programmer may have designed your own search engine. In most other cases, the choices come down to:

- downloading a free search engine from the web
- buying a special search engine package
- subscribing to a search facility provided by your Internet Service Provider (ISP)

Quite frankly, don't rely on the first option to provide a very useful service. In this business, like any other, you only get what you pay for. On the other hand, the last two options are usually quite efficient – as well as the most cost-effective in relation to programming your own. Moreover, if you are building a search-based site, obviously, your search engine has to be among the best available, so it makes sense to go to an outside expert who has a primary focus.

Typical search-engine problems

Although these are technical issues, information architects should be aware of the problems their site's visitors may face.

Perhaps the greatest problem is that most search engines simply cannot categorize information in any particularly useful manner. Users receive a long and often meaningless list of links. This is particularly true if someone has searched for several words and is told that a particular link has "78 percent" relevancy. Honestly, what does 78 percent of two words represent? Even worse, a search engine may come up with *no* results, even if a subject is represented on the site. As a consequence, visitors searching for a particular product will probably go away thinking that you cannot help them – which is disastrous! This is actually a very common problem since most search engines don't actually read the editorial content but merely index a list of keywords for each page and thus overlook important details. Worst of all, if the site is physically located on several different servers, the search engine may only examine the server from which it was accessed and come up empty-handed.

Here's a typical example: One of the "Big Three" American car manufacturers has a site split on to several individual servers. If you go into the homepage and search for their bestselling model, you won't find a single link! That's because the actual car information is on another server, where it functions as an independent subsite.

Certain database-generated sites (Lotus/Domino in particular) will invariably provide a lot of duplicate links, which visitors find incredibly annoying. There's also a risk that the search engine will provide convenient links to pages that are actually off-limits to the general public.

The use of frames also creates problems since virtually no search engines include the entire page in the link they've located. In other words, you may end up with a page of editorial content, but lack the related navigation bar. This is also a good reason to include a separate hypertext home link on each and every content page. By the way, this is one of the few instances in which I *like* the label "Home."

At the time of writing, there is only one search engine on the market that effectively solves *all* of these problems – and several others, too. It's called MondoSearch (mondosoft.com) and is well worth a closer look.

Remember, no matter which search engine you use, your visitors will probably appreciate a special page that tells them how to use it. Make sure to include this in your structure.

Keep in mind ...

- Secondary features are usually more functional in nature and are often grouped separately, not as part of the main menu.

- Don't call a page "Home" if it is an integral part of your navigational scheme.

- If a menu choice is going to open an e-mail window, make sure visitors *know* this before they click on the link.

- A site map is a supplement to existing navigation. It's not a substitute for *bad* navigational planning.

- Try to create a way in which returning visitors can easily locate the changes that have been made since their last visit.

- FAQ is *not* a miscellaneous section for all the bits and pieces you couldn't get to fit properly!

- If you need a search engine, buy a good package from a company that has their primary focus in this area. If you download something for free, you get what you pay for!

- If your site is located on multiple servers, make sure your search engine can index your *entire* site.

Refining the first structure

Since your last meeting with the web team, you've probably talked to most of the members individually to get their input on specific structural matters. The time has now come to present your proposed structure to the entire team. This is your big opportunity to explain how it hangs together and the reasons behind your decisions.

These meetings can either go extremely well or extremely badly, but oddly enough, the quality of the structure itself usually has little bearing on the outcome. The real problem occurs when people fail to see the site through the same eyes. If the head of sales still insists that all his customers *know* what an XJ-140 Super Widget does, or the head of engineering still claims that customers actually *understand* secret-society language, you may end up in the middle of a fight. However, if the initial meetings have been productive and you, as the information architect, have regularly talked to people along the way, your proposal should not contain any major surprises.

14.1 Input from the team

With a nice, neat structure in front of them (Figure 14.1) you'll find that all kinds of new information will suddenly come to light, or someone will get a bright idea as to a new function or feature that should be added. After all the long hours you've put in, it's tempting to reject many of these improvements out of hand – we information architects can become quite attached to our work. The point to bear in mind is this: *there is always more than one way to do things. There is never a "right" way*. So listen and remain flexible.

14.2 Reviewing the structure

At this point, the entire team should review the structure and ask the following questions.

Language
- Are we still talking to our primary target audience?
- Are our labels accurate and informative?

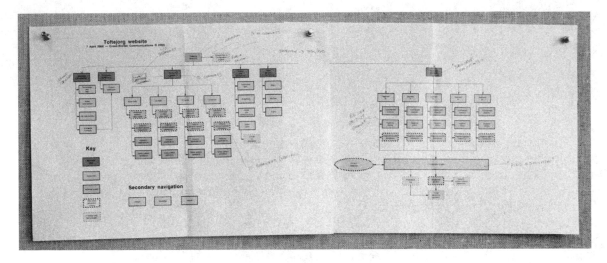

Figure 14.1 *This is the structure that resulted from the initial chunking shown on the whiteboard in Figure 4.1, the brochure review in Figure 4.2, and the manila folder structure shown in Figure 4.3. The handwritten notes were made during a preliminary meeting with the web team.*

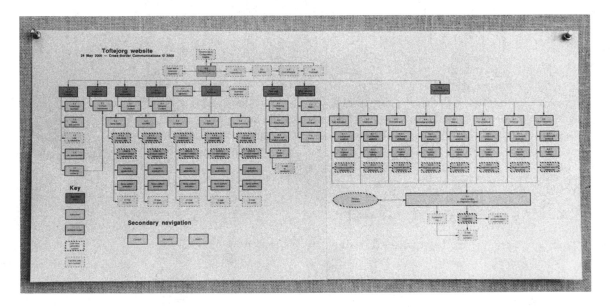

Figure 14.2 *The detailed structure as it was presented to the directors of the company, edited according to the needs identified by the web team during earlier meetings. It has since been revised several times.*

- Can any of our labels be misinterpreted?
- Are we speaking a language our audience understands?

Content

- Does all our information fit together logically?
- Can visitors easily (logically) find the answers to the questions we asked during the role-playing phase?
- Are any chunks of information left dangling somewhere without a logical place in the overall hierarchy?
- Is there a mechanism by which visitors can see what's new on our site? (If not, do we need one?)
- Have we effectively established shared references?
- Have we established ourselves as a company to be trusted?

Navigation and links

- Is our structure too wide? (Can some menus be consolidated effectively?)
- Is our structure too narrow and deep? (Do we need to split some menus up into more specific subjects?)
- Is there too much repetition of the same basic editorial content from one menu item to another?
- Can we reduce the number of clicks needed to reach the lowest levels without sacrificing understanding or logic?
- Are frequently accessed areas too far from the top level?
- Is related (contextual) information contained in different parts of the site properly linked? Is there a way to bundle it in an even more convenient way?

Individual pages

- Do we really have something to say on each of the main category pages or are they merely glorified menus?
- Have some pages been created merely for the sake of completeness?
- If someone has submitted information or placed an order, are all the appropriate "Thank you" pages indicated?

Goals and growth

- Does the structure live up to our primary goals?
- Is the site meeting the goals of our target audience?

- Have we given people a reason to come back and visit again?

- Is the site prepared for growth and/or change in the future?

- Have we found our site's USP? Is our product the hero?

Depending on the size of the site and the complexity of the information, this meeting can be as short as 20 minutes or may continue over the course of several days. Generally, though, if the team has prepared the groundwork carefully, most structures can be reviewed over the course of a few hours, particularly if decision-makers have had a chance to see earlier "work in progress." The information architect then retires to his or her office to change and edit the structure accordingly (see Figure 14.2).

A final note

In some cases, the team may decide that certain areas should be dealt with as separate subsites. Alternatively, there may be a need to create a site that more efficiently addresses the different needs of two or more audience profiles. These topics are discussed in the next two chapters. Sorry for any inconvenience – that's what happens when a subject needs to be presented in a linear fashion! Normally these decisions are made at a much earlier stage.

Keep in mind ...

- Listen to the rest of the web team. There is always more than one way to do things. There is never a "right" way.

- Review each of the points in the checklist carefully. Now is the time to settle any differences of opinion.

- Don't be afraid to make major changes if this will ultimately lead to a better website.

Building a subsite  15

15.1 Typical subsites

In essence, a subsite is just like a main website, with its own homepage, menu choices, navigation, and perhaps even style, but with one major difference: a subsite is almost always devoted to a much more specific topic or function. It's a very practical way to structure large, complex, informational universes and helps visitors focus on what *they* are interested in within the larger site framework. For example, a major hotel chain may have a main site focused primarily on general issues related to their operations, finances, future plans, etc. This site will probably also list the chain's hotels (Figure 15.1), but each of these will usually be linked to its own specific subsite containing practical contextual information for travellers: city maps, pictures of rooms and suites, prices, and perhaps even an online booking feature (Figure 15.2). These "local" sites may also offer a choice of languages.

Subsites will typically be "open" to all visitors or "closed" to limit access to a specific group. More about these in a moment. In the meantime, here are some examples of typical subsites:

- Subsidiary sites
  - basic business presentation (open)
  - information *for* subsidiaries (closed)
    - wholesale pricelists
    - training materials

- Local distributor sites
  - basic business presentation (open)
  - information *for* distributors (closed)
    - wholesale pricelists
    - training materials

- Key customer sites (closed)
  - transactions and order tracking

- Key supplier sites (closed)
  - information *for* suppliers
  - inventory management

Figure 15.1

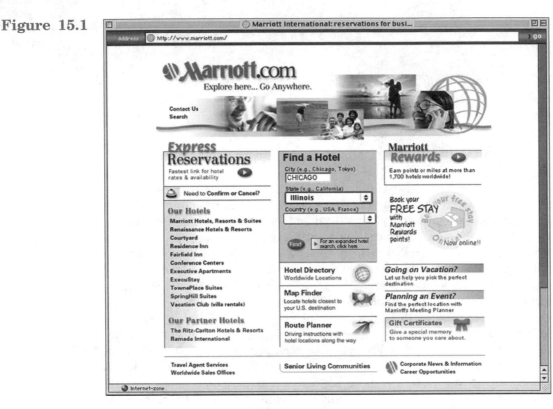

The homepage of Marriott.com prominently features a search engine to help visitors find a specific hotel.

- Local language sites (open)
- Special-interest sites, such as:
  - segmented typical customer profiles (open)
  - press lounge (open or closed)
  - investor relations forum (open or closed)
  - technical forum/chat (open or closed)

15.2 When do you need a subsite?

In general, you should consider building a subsite if:

- information is *only* of interest to one very specific target group within the spectrum of all possible visitors
- there is sufficient information to justify a subsite for this group

Figure 15.2

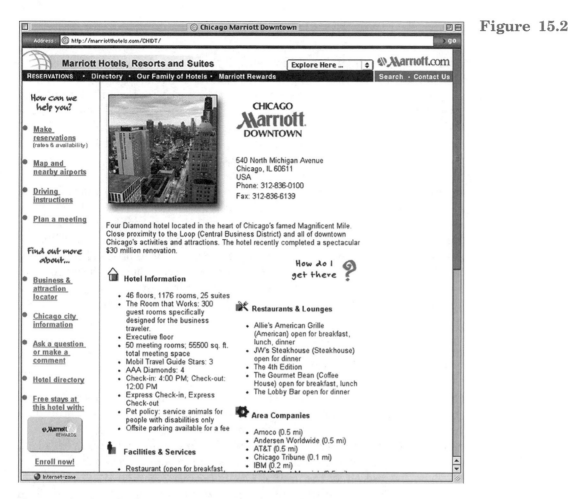

Once you've found a hotel you like, Marriott provides a host of helpful contextual links, such as restaurants and local attractions, maps and driving directions, and naturally, online booking.

- there is a need to segregate information for security purposes
- segregation will make the visitor feel important

Just to clarify things, a manufacturer of automobile tires will probably not want to create a subsite for each and every make of car. However, if the company has a special range of tires for off-road vehicles, this might qualify for a subsite. Alternatively, an international organization may want to create subsites in several major languages that more or less mirror the main site.

15.3 Accessing the subsite

Although hyperlinks from lower-level pages on the main site may be appropriate for accessing specific subsites for subsidiaries, distributors, etc., in most cases, a subsite should be accessible from the highest possible level of the main site. This is because the rules of informational detail are the same for both the subsite and the main site. Let me explain.

Imagine that our tire manufacturer's main site requires visitors to click three times to get to off-road tires. Suddenly, a link to the subsite whisks them off into an entirely new world, with new goals and newly segmented topics. Invariably there will be a jump backwards in terms of detail which may cause confusion and will probably irritate the visitor. As such, it's probably in everybody's interest to make this subsite accessible from the main page (although not necessarily from the main menu – a dynamic billboard listing may suffice). A splash on a subpage dealing with off-road tires might be a good supplement, as long as this splash clearly indicates that it links to an entirely different site. By the way, when people know they've just entered a new site (even a subsite) their built-in "click counter" usually resets itself.

15.4 Reusing information

In general, it's not a good idea to force visitors to hop back and forth between your main site and your subsite too often. Let's say you have structured all your product information along the lines indicated in Chapter 11 and have carefully coordinated the levels of detail. Now, you've decided to add a subsite devoted to some particular topic which needs to provide information for some, but not all, of the products described on the main site.

It's tempting to link the subsite back to the relevant product pages on the main site to avoid duplication, but this isn't always as clever as it seems. The whole advantage of a subsite is that it gives you a unique forum in which you can present your information and arguments. As such, you may find yourself stuck with levels of detail dictated by the main site that don't suit your current needs. In other words, don't cut yourself off from a great chance to customize your editorial content.

If you are producing subsites for an overseas subsidiary, you'll also have to contend with problems of language, which may make reuse of editorial content difficult. For example, English usage and spelling are *not* the same in the United Kingdom, the United States, Australia, New Zealand, Canada, South Africa, etc. Also, foreign-language sites work much better if *all* the pages are written in the same language. Sites that hop back and forth between two languages can drive you crazy – even if you speak both of them!

Finally, whatever you do, if there's any reason to believe that visitors may choose *not* to enter your subsite, don't cut them off from important information while they're browsing through your main site. That's also why your search engine needs to index your subsite as well as the main site.

15.5 Reusing design and navigation

If you do need to refer back to the main site regularly, you'll probably want to retain as much of the original design and navigation as possible so users do not become confused. In sites for subsidiaries, drawing on the same visual design sends a strong signal to visitors that the individual companies are part of a single, unified organization. That said, visitors are usually helped tremendously if they *know* that they have entered a special subsite and *know* when they've left it again. This isn't really a structural issue, but I felt it was worth mentioning anyway.

15.6 When to create new design and navigation

A hotel chain, for example, will probably develop a new structure for the individual hotels since the needs of visitors will normally be quite different from those coming to the main site. In this case, the subsite will feature a completely new set of menu options and possibly even a new design.

Often, a subsite can be designed so that it becomes a major attraction because of the site's specialized content and not just because of the products or services provided. For example, our off-road subsite for the tire manufacturer could be made attractive to *all* off-road enthusiasts by including useful information about rallies, meetings, and vehicle maintenance – perhaps even an online driving school. All of this, of course, is designed to encourage the visitor to come back again, increase the tire company's share of mind, and ultimately their sales.

Occasionally, detailed technical specifications may not need to be customized for a particular audience in relation to similar pages on the main site. In these cases, though, it's best to duplicate the content and reformat the page to match the style of the subsite so visitors don't get confused or lost. These pages should be specifically indicated on the structural diagram rather than simply by drawing a link to a similar page on the main site.

15.7 Adapting existing information from a CD-ROM

If the site owner already has other electronic presentations, the information architect is often called on to integrate these in a website. Basically, the information architect has two choices:

- to add the multimedia program as a separate subsite;
- to restructure and edit the multimedia program to fit the needs of the site.

In actual practice, it's usually difficult to simply "plug in" a separate multimedia production. If a CD or disk-based production was originally designed as a slide-show presentation, the linear aspects will almost always irritate visitors. On the other hand, if the CD features extensive use of video or very sophisticated navigation, these may not be suitable for use on the web for technical reasons. Finally, the production tools used to generate more traditional multimedia aren't always the same as those for the web, which may entail expensive reprogramming. When this happens, the site owner, the technical staff, and the information architect need to decide if it's really worthwhile to recreate the original program or to use the resources to create something new instead.

In most cases, the information architect will be called on to examine the multimedia program and adapt specific portions of the program to meet lower-level needs. Only rarely will an older multimedia presentation make its way to a website intact.

15.8 Guided tours

Guided tours aren't really subsites, but since they are unique entities that fall outside the normal site navigation, I've included them here. Although some sites feature guided tours for first-time visitors, this is usually an unnecessary aid. On the other hand, specific products and services may lend themselves to this kind of linear presentation (Figure 15.3). For

Figure 15.3

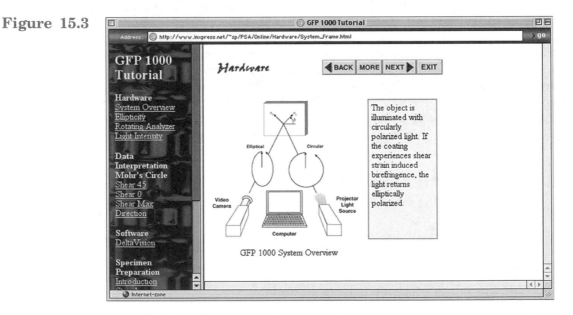

Online tutorials such as this one from Stress Photonics, help explain complicated technical issues – in this instance, thermoelastic stress analysis. Note that the contextual choices have been conveniently grouped in the main content area.

example, a software house may want to provide online step-by-step guidance as to how to set up and configure the product. Or a moving company might want to show people how to pack their dishes. There are lots of possibilities.

For the most part, you can insert guided tours anywhere in your structure, regardless of the level, as long as visitors have been exposed to the information necessary in order to understand them properly. Although you don't have to think about how many clicks it took visitors to find these tours, the tour itself probably shouldn't have more than four or five steps, supplemented by explanatory orphaned hyperlinks if necessary. Finally, make sure your visitors can leave any time they want (Figure 15.4) – don't force them to watch the whole show.

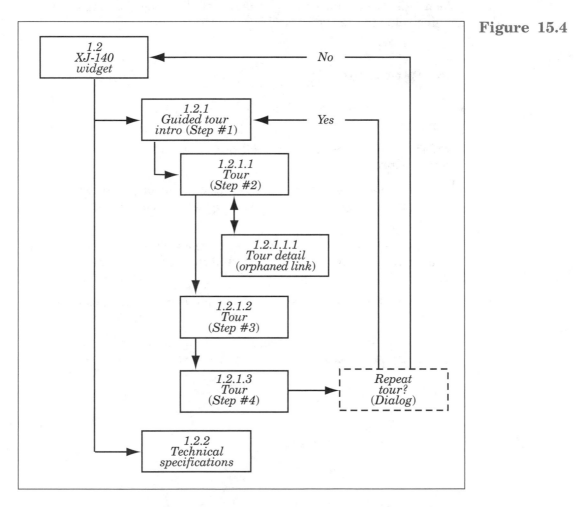

Figure 15.4

A diagram of a typical tour. Note that the linear steps 2–4 are considered subpages of Step 1, which helps preserve the integrity of the numbering system.

15.9 Providing real value

Visitors like to think they're special, which is one of the reasons some subsites require registration before people can enter a particular area. Many "closed" press lounges operate this way. Not only is it valuable for the site owner to find out which publications are interested in the company, but journalists like the feeling that they're getting information that is beyond the reach of the general public.

There's just one important rule to remember: if you're going to ask someone to give up their anonymity, you'd better give them something in return. There's nothing worse than receiving a password key only to discover that there is nothing of value behind the door! In fact, this is the golden rule of *all* subsites (open and closed): a subsite has to provide genuine value to the visitor.

Keep in mind ...

- Subsites are almost always devoted to a fairly specific topic or function.

- Subsites can be "open" or "closed" according to the needs of the visitor and/or site owner.

- If you have a "closed" subsite, make sure the inconvenience to the visitor is offset by the value of the information that can now be accessed.

- Make sure visitors know they have entered a specific subsite so they can get their navigational bearings and reset their internal "click counters."

- If your visitors will probably hop back and forth between your main site and the subsite, it helps if the designs of the sites are similar.

- Guided tours are *linear* presentations of individual topics. Make sure you give your visitors an exit if they don't want the full tour.

Talking to a specific audience

Sometimes, the web team will find that it has several well-defined target audiences with similar, but not identical needs. For example, a paint manufacturer may have both homeowners and professional contractors as customers. A bank may choose to differentiate between private individuals and businesses. In these (and other) cases, it can be worthwhile to create a site that can be adjusted to meet the different needs of different audience profiles.

Alternatively, the site owner may want to improve the experience of returning visitors.

Whatever the case, the aim is to create a site that quickly responds to a visitor's specific needs by increasing the percentage of relevant links to which the visitor is exposed, usually in terms of better contextual navigation. There are several ways to accomplish this:

- create a single, depth-segmented site
- create several profiled sections or subsites
- ask questions along the way to surface user-relevant information
- provide automatic adaptive navigation

In all instances, the goal is to provide the most personal service possible. The first two choices represent general *segmentation*, whereas the last two represent true *personalization*. By the way, there's a fine-line difference between customization and personalization. Customization generally means that the *visitor* does something to the site. Personalization means that the *site* itself adapts to the specific needs of an individual visitor.

16.1 Building one-to-one relationships

"One-to-one" is one of the latest buzzwords to hit the marketing scene. All it means is that you should treat each customer on an individual basis according to their knowledge and needs. For example, a car salesperson will quickly size up each individual sales situation and won't waste time pushing a sports car to a family of four. In other words, one-to-one is not a question of what *customers* want, but rather what does *this* customer want.

Figure 16.1

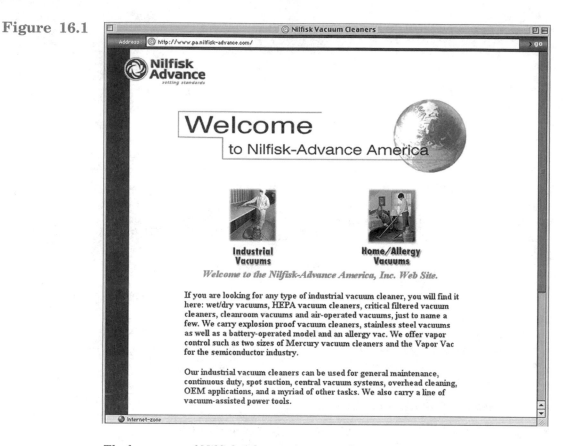

The homepage of Nilfisk-Advance America effectively divides visitors into two key target audiences.

Because of the web's interactive nature, it's a terrific tool for building these valuable relationships. But the web isn't as good as people sometimes imagine for one simple reason: it's very difficult to create a site that accurately anticipates and meets each and every individual need (Figure 16.1). You cannot see your visitors and it's often difficult to get them to tell you who they are. No matter how you tackle the problem, it takes a lot more energy (=money) to maintain a sophisticated multi-target site.

Let's take a closer look at some of the techniques involved in each of the options listed above.

16.2 Creating a depth-segmented site

A static, depth-segmented site builds on the basic principle that after two or three clicks, the visitor has essentially told the site owner something about his or her background and needs. Let me explain.

Figure 16.2

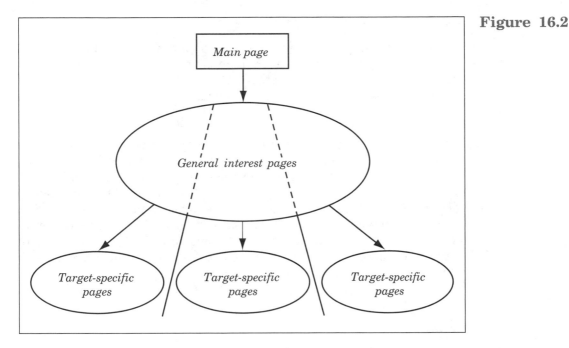

A generic diagram of a depth-segmented site. By the time visitors have drilled down to the target-specific pages, they can be more or less segregated in terms of navigation from the other site audiences.

If a visitor is deep inside your Technical FAQ, it's reasonable to assume that this person is a technician or some other serious user of your products. By the same token, a visitor reading the online version of your financial statement probably has an understanding of business and economics. A visitor reading about thrust coefficients is probably an engineer.

In terms of structure, the first few levels are structured to appeal to a broad audience. In other words, we structure our information so that ordinary visitors won't feel a need to venture beyond the third level. After about the third click, however, the editorial content of the site changes in that we *assume a degree of expertise* on the part of visitors that enables them to understand professional terminology. Peer-to-peer communication on the lower levels is the key difference between a depth-segmented site and an ordinary site. On and after the fourth level, a depth-segmented site usually starts to resemble a special subsite for a specific target audience. Design-wise, there will often be significantly increased emphasis on local and contextual navigation rather than on the main menu divisions.

Advantages and disadvantages

A static, depth-segmented site has one significant advantage over all others: it's easy to maintain since there is no duplication of information from one visitor profile to another. Also, editorial content for most of these more detailed pages can be provided directly by the site owner with significantly less need for professional editing.

Although in an ideal world, a professional writer would edit everything that is published on the site, in practice, this rarely happens. However, by about the fourth level in a depth-segmented site, one expert will be communicating with another expert, in which case *content* is more important than *style*. This is, of course, no excuse for bad writing, but it's easier to forgive unpolished prose here than it is on higher levels.

Depth-segmentation, though, is less successful if the basic sales argumentation needs to vary a great deal from one profile to the next. In general, business-to-business sites are better suited to this type of architecture than more commercial sites, simply because target audiences for business-to-business sites can be defined more accurately and the needs of visitors better anticipated.

16.3 Profiled subsites

Usually this works by asking the visitor to choose from a list of several possible profiles, each of which takes them to a new section or subsite created specifically to meet their needs (Figure 16.3). This often takes place on the main page, and almost never lower than two clicks off the first screen. Basic background information, such as company history, etc., may be repeated verbatim from site to site, as well as very technical lower-level pages.

By the way, if your organization's products are radically different for each audience, many of the problems listed in the following will be fairly minor. I'm assuming, though, that you are essentially promoting similar or identical products to audiences with significantly different needs – which is much more difficult.

Advantages and disadvantages

Since you are, in essence, creating new sites for each of your target audiences, you can vary the sales arguments and basic thrust of each site accordingly and provide some degree of site customization. This is a great advantage, but it often comes at a heavy cost in terms of site maintenance: each time a page needs to be updated in one profile, the chances are, there will be similar pages that must be updated in the other profiles as well.

Having monitored several sites of this type over the course of the past few years, I've come to the conclusion that even large companies have

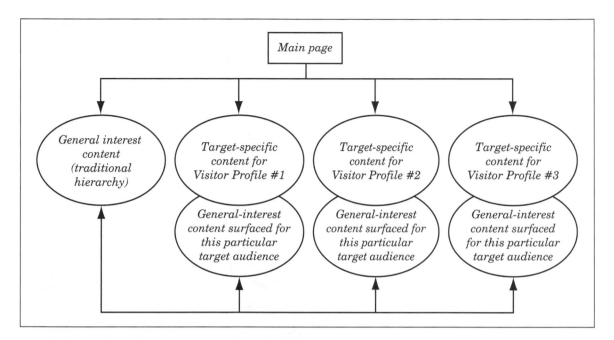

Figure 16.3   *This site has been structured to meet the needs of three distinct audience profiles, although a traditional hierarchy is also available for those who just want to browse around. Individual pages within the general hierarchy are contextually linked to the target-specific content. In theory, the general hierarchy could be completely hidden from view since its main function is to avoid having to create identical general-interest pages for each target audience.*

trouble maintaining profiled subsites. Many sites that once provided well-differentiated editorial content now feature pretty much the same information, repeated three or four times with only minor differences. If you choose this method, make sure you're really willing to take on the long-term responsibility. For larger companies with an extensive assortment of products and services, this usually entails hiring a full-time staff member to maintain the site properly.

Another problem with sites of this nature is that visitors often worry that they will be cut off from subjects that are not discussed in their selected profile. Moreover, the site owner loses out on what I call the "encyclopedia effect." This is what happens when you look up a subject in a reference book (or even the Yellow Pages) and find something else of interest along the way that has no relation to the subject you're actually looking for. This is serendipity in its most basic form. On business-to-business sites, serendipity is less important than it is on hardcore business-to-consumer e-commerce sites since e-commerce site owners need to encourage a higher degree of impulse shopping. Anyway, deciding what to put in the individual profiles is always more difficult than you first think.

To eliminate duplication of general-interest information, many sites ask visitors to choose a particular profile only with regard to a specific topic. A typical (though not particularly elegant) solution is simply to provide menu choices such as:

Our XJ-140 Super Widget is the perfect solution for a wide range of specific widget needs:

Are you an <u>engineer</u>?

Are you an <u>architect</u>?

Are you a <u>programmer</u>?

Are you a <u>designer</u>?

Remember, though, this is merely customized segmentation, *not* personalization.

Alternatively, if the basic benefits of your products and services can be discussed in a series of segment-related upper-level pages, it may not be necessary to produce segmented product pages on the lower levels, too. In other words, your segmented pages lead to generic product pages that highlight general features and benefits. That said, as the selection of products for any given target segment will often vary, it's often useful to store the generic data in a database. This lets you generate dynamic product pages within the hierarchy of the individual segment without the need to send visitors to a static page located under a different menu heading, or create copies of the static page in several locations. It's difficult to maintain numerous identical pages; by using a database, you only have to make changes once.

16.4 Asking questions

One of the most obvious ways to determine a visitor's interests is to simply ask relevant questions right from the start. A search type site essentially performs this service by asking "What do you want to know?" and letting visitors type in appropriate queries. Alternatively, the website itself can ask a series of questions in order to provide some degree of customization. CNN.com does this when it asks visitors what they'd like to appear on their main menu.

Another approach is to use what experts call "collaborative filtering," which represents true personalization. This is what Amazon.com does when it prepares lists of book recommendations. By asking visitors specific questions regarding likes and dislikes, the site can quickly steer people to books that may interest them. Moreover, Amazon also tracks the books the visitor has purchased in the past and adds this information to its database and compares it to data from other customers. If you have bought the same two or three books as Customer A, Amazon assumes you might be interested in a fourth book that Customer A also bought. This is really what "collaborative filtering" is all about.

Advantages and disadvantages

The obvious advantage is that people actually tell you what they've come for. If you use this information correctly, you will invariably create a more useful site, enhance the visitor's online experience, and build customer loyalty. Generally, you have to ask your questions early on if you really expect to personalize the site. If you ask questions at a lower level, you might as well provide ordinary menu options.

The main disadvantage is that except for searching, these techniques frequently assume the visitor plans on coming back, which isn't always the case. Probably, about the worst thing you can do is to start a website experience by asking people to fill in a long questionnaire. It's the single most effective way to scare away first-time visitors.

Apart from removing a visitor's anonymity (which can be a major psychological hurdle in itself) many people fear you'll use their answers to invade their privacy or compromise their computer's security. Moreover, many visitors will not let you post a "cookie" on their computer. A cookie is simply a small file containing some text or numbers that helps a site identify a particular visitor (or at least their computer) so it can make adjustments according to their past preferences. As people are scared of viruses and other Trojan horses, many users simply deny websites the right to put anything on their hard disks. The only real option for these folks is to sign in each time they come to a site. Not everyone is willing to do so. Of course, it's also possible to ask people to bookmark specially created pages, but this short-circuits security since there is no user-authentication.

Even if you *can* get visitors to part with preference information, without actually revealing personal details, you also have to give them something back in terms of enhanced functionality so they feel their efforts were worthwhile. Remember, you need to have a pretty big site before you can truly generate useful custom menus and pages for all your visitors. Moreover, if you can't tag the visitor with a cookie or by some other method, the information they've given you can only be used during the course of a single user session.

Straightforward menu customization as practiced by CNN.com is more innocuous, but only really works in a newsletter-style environment. Again, you have to provide a wide selection of choices before visitors will feel a real need to weed out the unwanted links.

The main disadvantage of collaborative filtering is that it requires a great deal of raw data and sophisticated software to process it. In general, this technique is best-suited to sites that provide a wide range of homogeneous choices (books, CDs, etc.), but it is a very effective tool when used and maintained properly.

Corporate search engines can be very useful if people know what they're looking for. That said, if visitors don't really understand the scope of your site, they may come away empty-handed and disappointed. One of the ways around this is to force visitors to structure their queries by using a controlled vocabulary list. In other words, you only let them search for pre-defined subjects and functions for which there always is an answer. You might want to refer back to the discussion of customized online museums in Chapter 5. For a brief review of the many problems related to search engines in general, see Chapter 13.

16.5 Adaptive navigation

Basically, what happens is that the website monitors what a visitor has clicked on, and revises the navigational options (usually contextual) according to what the site thinks a visitor is interested in. For the most part, this means that after a number of clicks, the site will "tag" the visitor as belonging to a particular profile and automatically show the screens targeted to this group. Generally, the software used to generate these navigational models is supplied by a third-party vendor: Net Perceptions (netperceptions.com), BroadVision (broadvision.com), and Vignette Corp. (vignette.com) are three of the current industry leaders and all are major suppliers of collaborative filtering software.

Advantages and disadvantages

The primary advantage is that this kind of "personalization on-the-fly" is invisible to the visitor. Of course, a certain number of clicks are required to determine user preferences, so there's always the risk that a visitor will leave before the site has figured out what this person wants. (Interestingly enough, both BroadVision and Vignette Corp. wanted me to fill in questionnaires during my first online visits.)

It's still a little early to tell just how effective this technique is since relatively few sites seem to be using it. Moreover, as it is invisible, you never really know if your visit is being personalized or not. At any rate, a lot of work is being done in this field and it's worth keeping the technique in mind. That said, the problems of generating and maintaining profiled editorial content will probably always be around, no matter how sophisticated the software.

For the most part, click tracking is much more useful to the site owner than it is to individual visitors since it provides quite a bit of useful information about general user preferences. NetGenesis (netgenesis.com) has some particularly effective tracking tools. However, the further use of this information in terms of sales and marketing (on and off-line) is beyond the scope of this book.

Keep in mind ...

- Segmentation according to specific target audiences helps surface user-relevant information.

- Customization means the visitor does something to the site. Personalization means the site adapts to the needs of an individual visitor.

- Sophisticated multi-target sites generally have high maintenance costs if they are to remain effective after the launch.

- Depth-segmentation doesn't work very well if the basic sales argumentation varies greatly from one audience to the next.

- Profiled subsites are easier to maintain if target-specific pages are kept to a minimum without repeating information of more general interest.

- Don't scare off your visitors by suddenly confronting them with a long questionnaire.

- First-time visitors generally don't like to have to give up their anonymity.

- Adaptive navigation requires visitors to have spent some time exploring a fairly large site before it becomes truly effective.

17 Moving on to the production phase

One happy day, you'll suddenly discover that all the pieces of your informational jigsaw puzzle have fallen neatly into place. You're pleased with the result and so are the other members of the web team. Now, armed with the finished structure, your team can move on to the really exciting phase: designing and assembling the site.

In truth, a structure is never really finished. That's because a website is a dynamic tool, prepared for growth and designed for change – and the changes will come sooner than you expect. Don't let structural adjustments at this point frustrate you. They don't necessarily mean you didn't do a good job the first time around, rather, they give you a chance to do things even better as new ideas and opportunities arise.

17.1 The production phase

Most structures start changing in subtle ways almost as soon as the first design sketches are produced. Ideally, the information architect has been working closely with a graphic designer and usability expert throughout the initial phase, and perhaps even with a special designer called in to create the navigation. Nevertheless, when things start to appear on a real computer screen, with real links and real graphics, you may discover that the structure, navigation, and overall graphic design don't blend as well as everyone had hoped. Although these may be three *distinct* issues, you don't want your site's visitors to perceive them as *separate* issues.

Keep in mind, the designer is just as interested in creating a well-functioning site as you are. At this point, the aesthetic values we ignored earlier become tremendously important. Although it's fair to put up a fight if the designer insists on an idiotically small typeface or is about to commit some other gaff that will seriously jeopardize the site's functionality, don't get into silly squabbles about other issues that are really only a matter of taste. This is a common problem since the information architect frequently comes to think of the site as his or her own personal project. In other words, if the designer wants the background to be yellow, don't waste time arguing that it should be light blue. Ideally, there will be an opportunity to conduct usability tests (see Chapter 18) – the results of which will provide valuable objective data to help everyone involved move beyond subjective guesswork.

17.2 Where designers and architects clash: labels

Information architects and designers invariably disagree regarding the length of labels. Information architects like to provide as much information as possible, designers usually want things short and sweet. To be perfectly honest, I cannot remember having worked on a site without this issue coming up at some point. There is only one solution to this problem: compromise.

Talk things through with the designer and explain why you chose the labels you did. Investigate other ways of displaying the menu choices. Consider any possible label alternatives. Whatever you do, don't think that your way is the only way! Hopefully, you have enough aesthetic sense to understand the designer's dilemma, and the designer is willing to respect the communicative aspects of the labels. Whatever the problem, though, I assure you, *there's always a workable solution you both can live with*. You just have to be willing to look for it.

17.3 Working with content providers

In more than a few cases, the information architect will also be a key content provider, at least for information on the first two or three levels. Alternatively, the information architect may be responsible for editing the work of others.

However, if you aren't directly involved in supplying the editorial content, you must talk to those who are. It's important that these people are properly introduced to the overall structure before they start submitting actual text. Content providers need to understand the overall goals of the site and know who they are talking to on any given page. If you've put together a set of content descriptions, as suggested in Chapter 9, be sure to explain what these documents represent and how they are to be used.

Of course, it's not necessarily your job to keep the content providers on a tight rein – if anyone is going to do so, it will probably be the site's editor. In any event, content providers should probably be given a bit of leeway in their work. That's because they are always the first to spot pages that are superfluous or suggest better ways to present information on the lower levels. They may also discover important chunks of information that were overlooked earlier. That said, when these new chunks are discovered, the information architect needs to help define their proper location within the overall scheme of things. Many successful websites have become confusing because they suffer from having "too many cooks." As always, though, theory is one thing, putting things into practice is something else entirely.

Throughout this phase, one of the information architect's most important jobs is to keep the structure or site map up to date. Once the production starts in earnest, it's easy to forget to incorporate the changes that will occur. When the site is expanded or changed (or merely evaluated) in the months to come, your structural blueprint will provide a key visual aid.

Keep in mind ...

- A structure is never really finished. Changes will continue to take place throughout the production phase.

- Changes give you an opportunity to do things even better.

- Structure, navigation, and graphic design may be distinct issues, but visitors must not experience them as such.

- Don't get into fights with the designer regarding aesthetic details unless these issues will jeopardize usability.

- Make sure the editorial content providers understand the informational goals of each page.

- Editorial content providers will be the first to discover structural problems. Listen to what they have to say!

- On the other hand, don't let your site lose its focus through the well-intentioned efforts of "too many cooks."

Testing the usability  18

The old cliché, "the customer is always right," is particularly relevant when it comes to creating websites. Having spent weeks or months putting together a site, it's very tempting to think that visitors are stupid because they can't find their way around your superbly structured site. Usually, you first discover these navigational problems when you get a friend to sit down with you and surf around a site you've helped put together. "Just click on the red thing!" I hear you cry in frustration. Or "Why didn't you simply use the button over there?" Although this little trial isn't particularly organized, and at this stage you may not be willing to admit that something is amiss, what you are experiencing forms the essence of *usability testing*.

18.1 What it's all about

Usability testing consists of finding test subjects (preferably four or more people from your target audience) and asking them to answer questions or solve problems (usually task-based) that draw on information they can find on the website. While they work at the computer, the observer sits and watches what they do, encouraging test subjects to think out loud, helping put them at ease, and providing moral support and guidance without actually helping to solve the specific problem at hand. Often a video camera, focused on the screen, is used to record both the comments and mouse movements.

Typical tasks for test subjects include basic factfinding (e.g. What is the company's phone number?); comparisons (e.g. Which products have a specific feature?); and evaluations (e.g. Is it easy to order a product?). Other tasks may relate to more general site functionality such as the quality and ease of use of the search engine or a process-oriented feature such as online purchasing.

One of the most important functions of the observer is to note the test subject's basic computer ability, thus providing valuable information regarding the computer-literacy of this individual – and by extension, the target audience. For example, is this person double-clicking on hyperlinks (they only need to be clicked once). Or, do pop-ups and drop-down menus cause confusion? The observer also makes a record of the test subject's ability to find things on the screen (design ergonomics). Of even greater importance, the observer will note how test subjects *react* to the site. Are they *surprised* by what appears on a new page? Are they *relieved* when they have finally solved a problem? Are they *confused* by the available choices? Are they *frustrated* by their lack of choices or their inability to complete some process?

The incredible value of usability testing is that it doesn't rely on your own "best guess" as to how people will respond, it's based on first-hand observation and dialog. Furthermore, test subjects will invariably come up with numerous useful suggestions as to how the site can be improved. Unfortunately, most usability testing occurs far too late in the production process – if it is performed at all. Ideally, impartial tests should be carried out at various intervals throughout the development process.

Impartial, though, is a key word in this regard. The observer must avoid asking leading questions that provide clues as to how a problem may be solved. Moreover, test setups are usually fairly unnatural, which may cause some test subjects to react differently than they would in the privacy of their own home or office. Thinking out loud in front of a video camera can be a very stressful experience.

Several excellent books have come out on this extremely important subject in recent years. You'll find them listed in the bibliography. The specific techniques (practical and psychological) of designing and conducting usability testing are extremely complex, but as an information architect, you must have a basic idea as to what it's all about. Here is a very brief tour of one of the most important areas of specialization in the web industry today.

The phrase, "Kids, don't try this at home" is particularly applicable here: people who have been directly responsible for the development of a site should not be conducting these tests – and there isn't nearly enough information here to do it properly anyway. Leave this to impartial experts!

18.2 **Heuristic evaluations**

Essentially, these are sessions in which one or more usability experts review a site (or paper prototypes) themselves and suggest improvements based on their own "best practice" experience and subjective opinions. These evaluations are always useful, but are particularly valuable during the early design stages when it's still easy and inexpensive to make major changes.

18.3 **Testing with pencil and paper**

Some very basic testing regarding the usability of your labels can be accomplished at a very early stage. Quite simply, test subjects are provided with a number of menu choices and a list of task-based questions. They are then asked them to write down which menu choice they think will bring them closer to the answer they seek.

For example, a set of menu choices for an "About the company" section might include:

- History
- Organization
- Research and development
- Quality control
- Sales and service
- Worldwide addresses

Armed with this information, test subjects might be asked to answer questions along the following lines:

- Where would you find last year's financial figures?
- Where would you find the e-mail address for the sales department?
- Where would you click if you wanted to apply for a job?

By reading through the responses, the test may show that people who wanted financial figures went to either "History" or "Organization" even though you *wanted* them to choose "History." And if the test includes a "Don't know" response option in the example above, you may discover that most respondents were unable to find a clearcut path to the information they wanted – particularly those looking for a job! In short, this kind of testing will help you, as an information architect, determine if you need to add extra menu choices or improve the scent of your labels, depending, of course, on the specific lower-level information you want people to find. Although this simple test doesn't require an electronic prototype of any kind, it's only really useful in judging the relative merits of various sets of labels.

18.4 Testing a simple navigational interface

If a graphic design has been created in which the individual web pages and the navigation is static (without drop-down menus, blinking buttons, or animated attention-getters) it's possible to take the pencil-and-paper technique a step further. By giving test subjects color prints of sample screens, they can circle the element or menu choice they think will best lead them to the required information. For the most part, the questions are similar to those used in the simple menu test mentioned previously, although if real editorial content is provided on these screen mock-ups, the questions can be a bit more specific.

In actual use, this kind of test will reveal more about whether people can *find* the needed link rather than whether the link's label is accurate. This is a sort of "poor-man's usability test" since it's always far more worthwhile to test a real electronic site. Quite simply, people react very differently in front of a screen than with a piece of paper. But if you're on a tight budget or the web team has serious disagreements about a preliminary design, this may help resolve some critical graphic issues. A heuristic evaluation, though, is very worthwhile at this stage.

18.5 Testing a structural prototype

Another possibility is to take the basic structure and build a simple clickable prototype that contains no graphic elements, but does move the visitor to a new page each time a link is activated. In this instance, volunteers are asked questions designed to test their ability to find specific low-level pages.

The individual pages don't need to have any editorial content apart from a headline or page title so the test subject has some basic frame of reference. Also, if some links will be physically grouped together on the finished site, try to keep them grouped in the prototype, too. At any rate, by observing the places in which test subjects are forced to back up because they made the wrong choice or got confused, it's easy to spot the menus that are ambiguous or misleading.

Using a site generator such as Microsoft FrontPage, a structural prototype can usually be put together in an hour or two and can be extremely useful, particularly in the early stages of site development. In fact, even if you can't afford to call in outside test subjects, if you click through the prototype yourself, you'll often spot problems you didn't see on paper. For example, if your structure forces visitors to pogo-stick back and forth between levels, you'll soon find out. Alternatively, if you've offered visitors too many non-homogeneous menu choices, these too will become much more visible.

18.6 Testing a complex navigational interface

The more sophisticated the design, the greater the need to test the basic mechanics of getting around the site. This is particularly true if the navigation makes extensive use of drop-down menus, rollovers or special graphic buttons in the main content area. Although this type of test is most helpful when fine-tuning the design, the information architect can also learn a lot during this process, which is why I mention it now.

In this case, the prototype is fully functional in terms of navigation and has all its graphics in place. However, the site has little or no editorial content – only the basic page headlines, plus blocks of typeset gibberish to mark where the actual written content will be placed. If the finished site will feature hyperlinks within the main content area, these also need to be functional.

The test subject is seated in front of a computer and sets out to find answers to various questions. In addition to the basic "where would you find" questions, since the prototype has all its navigation, the test person can also be asked more specific content questions such as "Does this company have an office in New York?" or functionality questions such as "Is it easy to order products?"

As always, the observer's job is to see if the test subject uses the site as it was designed to be used, and note when someone runs into problems finding the right buttons to click. Although the observer may coach the test subject, particularly if someone gets "dead-ended" and cannot figure out how to get back to a previous page or the main menu, it's often best to let people try and sort things out for themselves. If people get stuck, you want your test to indicate *where*, you want to know *why*, and you want to know *how* they try to solve the problem.

18.7 Full-blown beta-testing

A "beta" version of any computer software product (including a website) is one that is fully functional, has its proper content, but hasn't yet been released. In other words, it's a test version that provides one last chance prior to the launch to fix anything that doesn't work correctly from a programming standpoint, is confusing from a design standpoint, or misunderstood from a structural standpoint.

The test setup is the same as for navigational testing (video camera, etc.) but this time, two more types of question can be added to the list. Since most, if not all of the editorial content is in place, it's possible to ask test subjects to make comparisons and judgments. For example, they can be asked to find out which products have a specific feature, or whether the company seems trustworthy. This means the test subject needs to do a lot of clicking around to come up with an answer and it's the observer's job to see whether or not this happens efficiently.

Remember, as far as possible you'll want to find test subjects that belong to the proper target group. In other words, don't ask people in your own company to test the site, get real potential users. The fact is, using the web is still a new experience for many people, which means that what seems obvious to those who designed the site may confuse "average" users.

Keep in mind ...

- Usability testing is one of the most important aspects of professional website production.

- These task-based tests should ideally be conducted at regular intervals throughout the development process.

- Heuristic evaluations by usability experts provide valuable feedback regarding the generic usability of the site.

- You need to test actual members of the target audience – not just your colleagues in the office.

- Information architects are not the best people to carry out usability testing on their own sites. This should be left to impartial experts.

- Simple paper-based tests can show the information architect if labels are accurate and have the right scent.

- Structural prototypes can be used to identify navigational problems such as excessive pogo-sticking.

- During beta-tests of a nearly completed site, users can be asked to make comparisons and judgments in addition to factfinding.

- Usability tests provide hard facts. They don't depend on your own "best guess."

Looking forward

19

These days, any book on information architecture would be incomplete without touching on the subject of wireless internet. Also, there are quite a few practical and legal issues that will need to be addressed by information architects in the coming years.

A fair portion of what you'll read in this chapter is based on hard fact, but even so, much is simply my own speculation. Although I cannot claim to have a better crystal ball than anyone else, some of the trends appear clearly enough to warrant some discussion, so here goes.

19.1 The advent of WAP

Barely a year after the introduction of mobile phones featuring Wireless Application Protocol (WAP) capability, there are over a million European subscribers to WAP services; and according to the 1999 Annual Report from Lucent Corporation, 26 Americans sign up for similar services *each minute*. Half a world away during that same minute, 34 Chinese also sign up. Lucent is a major supplier of mobile internet solutions, so they ought to know!

Even so, the number of individual WAP services in any geographic market is still fairly easy to monitor. In many ways, the year 2000 is reminiscent of early 1995 – back when you could still count the number of individual sites on Yahoo. The boomtown atmosphere surrounding WAP also brings back memories of the first years of the web, complete with many grand predictions about how it's going to change our lives. Well ...

The jury is still out.

What is WAP?

WAP is an open communication standard that allows people to access dynamic content from mobile phones, Personal Digital Assistants (PDAs), and other highly portable devices most of us haven't even seen yet. The technology is complemented by numerous other innovations designed to increase wireless connectivity.

Bluetooth, for example, is an important new short-range radio technology that does away with the line-of-sight limitations of current infrared communications. Cisco Systems is working on microwave communication, and The Wireless Ethernet Compatibility Alliance (WECA) plans to become the wireless standard for homes and offices. In short, it's reasonable to assume that wireless connectivity will not be a major problem in the years to come.

Like HTML-based browsers, WAP also relies on URLs to find a site, but that's where the similarity ends. WAP accesses specially formatted data using a protocol known as WML, which is a subset of XML. Just for the record, WML stands for Wireless Markup Language – a scaled-down version of HTML; and XML stands for eXtensible Markup Language, which describes a class of data objects stored on computers called XML documents, and which, to some extent, also describes the behavior of the programs designed to process these objects.

For now, most WAP users access sites through special dial-in portals. As a result, the range of services to which users are exposed depends to some extent on what an individual service provider is willing to offer, not all of these services are free. By the way, don't confuse WAP phones with genuine browser telephones like the one Val Kilmer ran around with in the 1997 movie "The Saint." His Nokia 9000 Communicator actually lets users surf ordinary HTML websites (although the latest generation of communications are now WAP-enabled).

What can WAP do?

The most widespread WAP services include news, weather, sports results, stockmarket quotations, currency exchange rates, traffic information, airline and train schedules, and home banking. However, service providers are rapidly expanding the range of WAP options. For example, Telecom Italia now offers a restaurant guide, movie and TV schedules, and even lottery ticket sales. Not surprisingly, Yahoo, AltaVista, MSN, Amazon, and eBay are also practicing "m-commerce" these days. In fact, some experts say that pretty much everything on the web will soon be available. According to the Gartner Group, 80 percent of all new applications will be mobile phone enabled by 2004.

How does WAP work?

Since WAP data doesn't use HTML, special WML files must be created for WAP devices. Also, WML doesn't support hyperlinks in the traditional sense, so the hierarchy becomes much more visible than on a traditional website.

WAP information is divided into "decks" and "cards" – borrowing terminology from the old days of computer punch cards (see Figure 19.1). Decks can contain almost any number of individual cards (=pages), limited only by the current restriction of 3200 bytes per deck. Only one deck can be "open" (in memory) at a time. That said, some cards may contain

Figure 19.1

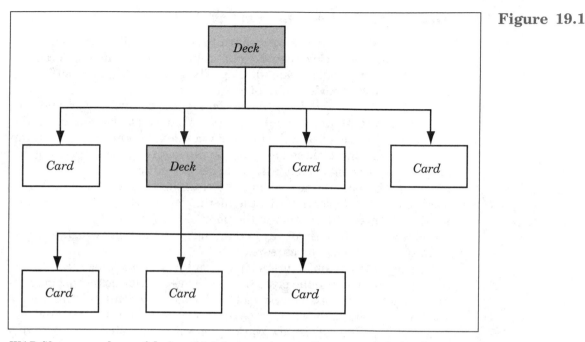

WAP files are made up of decks, which in turn can contain numerous individual cards. In order to create deeper structures, a card can trigger the opening of a new deck. However, only one deck is resident in the mobile device at any time.

instructions (a menu label) that open a new deck, thus permitting site designers to create deeper hierarchies. As memory is so limited, graphics are virtually non-existent except for the occasional logo or icon. Moreover, editorial content for individual cards is rarely longer than about 50 words. To avoid excessive scrolling, most menus are limited to about 3–8 topics. And finally, because WAP users are usually looking for specific information, many top menus actually function as simple indexes, for example, A–G, H–R, and S–Z, each of which opens a new deck.

It takes time to download new decks, so one of the basic tasks for the information architect is to make sure a user gets into the needed deck as quickly as possible. Not surprisingly, most WAP applications have a very shallow hierarchy for this very reason.

Although HTML and WML can reside on the same server, we really are talking about two parallel hierarchies that don't have much effect on each other – and probably don't even resemble each other. When a URL is accessed, the server notes the type of protocol needed and delivers the correct version of the site.

For those of you who are interested in seeing what WAP is all about (without actually having to buy a fancy phone), you can download a browser application called WinWAP (PC only) from www.slobtrot.com. This allows you to browse WAP sites from your PC.

Why surf on a five-line screen?

Most of the web developers I've talked to seem to think that WAP represents a giant step backwards: "No one wants to surf a cut-rate version of the web on a tiny liquid crystal display. The gear just isn't geared for this kind of activity!" They're right, of course.

Current phones and PDAs have limited computing power and tiny memories, the batteries run out quickly, the bandwidth is limited, the displays are far too small, and the input devices (apart from voice) are miserable. Let's be honest, these days, mobile phones are great for talking and PDAs make very nifty calendars – but that's about it.

Just don't make the mistake of ignoring the issue or thinking things aren't going to change. Already, the lifetime of my current phone battery is 100 times greater than that of the phone I bought seven years ago. And developers are well on their way to building look-and-blink eyeglasses that do away with screens and cursors.

Although PDA manufacturers have been lukewarm in their reception of WAP (probably because the protocol is so phone-centric), acknowledging the fact that internet access is practically non-existent when the PDA is away from the desktop PC, they too are looking for ways to improve their products. What's more, Microsoft is now working on so-called "microbrowsers" that can read standard HTML using the mobile phone's native operating system.

The point is, it's pointless to make any predictions about the future except to note that historically, whenever the times call for technological innovation, it usually takes place. I suspect that we're in for some roller-coaster years in our business.

19.2 What's the new role of the information architect?

To be perfectly frank, you'll probably be doing much the same as what you're doing today, but in a revised format. After all, most of the principles of information architecture are generic: the rules don't *change* as much as they *adapt* to embrace new technologies, WAP is just one of the current possibilities. As far as WAP is specifically concerned, important clues to as to what the future holds can be gained by examining the applications that already have a popular foothold. This helps identify some interesting common denominators.

To begin with, portable devices are just that – portable. People use them when they're on the go and the range of current applications reflects this need for fast access to specific information. Driving directions and telephone listings are natural applications (WAP also features some very basic global positioning capability so you won't get lost in strange cities).

High-rollers want to monitor their stocks and securities several times a day. Others want the security of an up-to-the-minute horoscope (which gives a whole new meaning to "reading palms"). But please note: in almost all instances, the individual chunks of information are both *small* and *specific* – and I think these kinds of chunks will continue to lie at the heart of future wireless applications. In the years to come, the job of the information architect will be to identify specific types of "need-to-know-*now*" information. My acronym for this is NKN.

As an information architect, you can often spot situations that would benefit from an NKN application when some event occurs that causes everyone around you to reach for their phones.

19.3 The death of the PC?

Are people really going to give up the advantages of larger computer screens for the convenience of smaller size? Some say yes, explaining that mobile phones are already outselling PCs by a factor of 2.5. But this is misleading. After all, PCs outsell cars by a similar factor and I don't think I'll be driving my laptop to work any time soon.

I believe the truly worthwhile wireless applications will be those that allow users to deal with NKN situations *when a PC is not at hand*. PCs will continue to be used when it is convenient to do so (although future computers will undoubtedly be smaller, lighter, and wireless). The mistake, though, is to assume that one generic device will supplant the other. After all, spoons and forks have not been replaced by Swiss Army knives.

19.4 The future of traditional websites

Although I made a big point of asking you to view your site as an *application* and to find your site's unique selling proposition back in Chapter 5, the differences between similar types of sites will invariably become harder and harder to spot in the coming years. As Jeffery Veen from Wired Digital has pointed out, most of today's portals are virtually indistinguishable without their logos. As a result, I suspect that "design and concept" in the traditional advertising sense may eventually provide differentiation for sites that otherwise have similar types of content and rate equally high in terms of usability. The lesson here? Don't fight with your designer!

The other main change will undoubtedly be the move from static HTML pages to dynamically generated pages drawing on database content. Today, most professional sites are already database driven, but I suspect that even the smaller homegrown sites will soon have this functionality. While there are many good reasons to incorporate databases, the most important of these by far is the need for more efficient content management.

19.5 Easier content-management interfaces

Site maintenance is a major headache for many smaller organizations that must outsource anything coded in HTML. Granted, most new word-processing programs can translate ordinary text files into HTML, but the trick is to get these online in an attractive and effective manner.

I fully expect that very soon, virtually all high-quality sites will come with some kind of easy-to-learn administration interface as part of the basic functionality. These interfaces (which will also require structure) will enable non-programmers to generate templated pages that follow the design guidelines of the site and automatically amend relevant menus when new pages are added. Up until now, most organizations that have felt a need for these kinds of content-management tools have commissioned their own proprietary applications.

The good news is that these interfaces should make updating a site much easier and therefore make the web in general a much more dynamic environment. The bad news is that it also makes it easier to take the information architect out of the loop. In fact, this has already happened in instances where, for example, copious Lotus Notes pages have been added to large corporate sites according to the personal whims of anyone with an access code.

I don't want to suggest that we, as information architects, should put the brakes on innovation, but clearly, we will have to carefully educate our respective masters in the value of our work so we maintain our professional mandates. In other words, a lot more of us are going to end up as policemen in cyberspace in an attempt to limit information anarchy, but this will only happen if our employers understand the problems involved. Let's face it, if we do our work well, it's invisible and therefore frequently underrated, ignored, or simply forgotten.

19.6 Better electronic tools for information architects

As individual web pages become more interactive through the use of rollovers, special controls for 3-D viewing, and other goodies such as collaborative filtering, the process of mapping out a site becomes much more complicated. As such, a great deal of work is being done these days to create multidimensional mapping tools that go far beyond the simple box-and-line diagrams of Visio and Inspiration. One of the more interesting companies working in this area is Vizbang (www.vizbang.com), although their products are still in the prototype phase.

For the time being, I'm still a great believer in flat drawings that can be displayed on an overhead projector or sketched on a whiteboard. My clients understand them, decision-makers don't need to power up a computer with special software to view them, and web teams can make notes in the margins. That said, I don't doubt the value of more sophisticated presentation methods, but I wonder if we really should be searching for a single, all-encompassing information architecture tool. We might actually be better off in the long run to supplement traditional two-dimensional diagrams with detailed content-provider sheets and electronic prototypes of the actual templates.

One of the areas, however, where better electronic tools are clearly needed is for mapping *existing* sites. More and more professional information architects are being asked to clean up older sites that have become unwieldly. These automatic site-mapping programs help create a current blueprint from which the information architect can gain the needed overview. Unfortunately, most current offerings fall far short of expectations. That said, you might want to take a look at PowerMapper from Electrum (www.electrum.co.uk), which is a low-cost utility that has done a surprisingly good job mapping static sites that I have personally architected (and hence have my own blueprint for comparative purposes).

19.7 Better window shopping

Throughout this book, I've more or less glossed over the fact that many sites are successful mainly because they are extremely entertaining. In the future, entertainment value will probably grow in importance as a differentiating factor for certain types of e-commerce sites. More specifically, I think that many information architects will be actively looking for ways to improve online window shopping. After all, an incredible number of people "shop" as a form of personal entertainment, even though they aren't really out to buy anything.

Right now, it's tough to window shop on the web – relatively few products are highlighted on each page and pictures are slow to load. The trick, I think, is to create online showcases that encourage more poking around with less clicking around. I don't have a specific solution, but I wish I did since whoever finds it is probably going to get rich. As bandwidth increases, new graphic possibilities will undoubtedly present themselves. Virtual reality is certainly one of the options, although the current virtual showrooms that build on a functional analogy of some sort are by and large disastrous.

19.8 The value of external links

In the future, single-owner sites (as opposed to portals, e-malls, etc.) will probably benefit from the ability to link to external sites featuring either related content or which appeal to the same general audience. From an information architect's point of view, Jakob Nielsen rightly notes that very few sites these days provide a natural point of entry that facilitates linking from other sites; the homepage may be too general a place to start. I think this is well worth keeping in mind. Conversely, many site owners worry that having exerted so much effort to get people to come to begin with, the last thing anyone should be doing is sending them off in a new direction. I have mixed feelings about this ...

The most important point to remember is that good links often provide real value to the user at very little cost to the owner. To be honest, an extensive and well-maintained links page is often the main reason I return to a particular site. By the way, the gimmick of opening a new browser window to encourage people to return probably does more harm than good. It confuses visitors and may give you a misleading impression of the time your visitors spend on your site.

19.9 **More effective use of metadata**

An incredible number of site owners still ignore the fact that most external search engines rely on metadata for proper indexing. With the explosive growth of the web, information architects are going to have to work much harder on their meta-titles, keywords, and descriptions if they expect visitors to find relevant pages on their sites.

Of course, there are many search engines that steadfastly refuse to index dynamically generated pages. So, the search-engine designers will have to get their acts together, too, if we are all going to bring the web to the next level.

19.10 **Keeping websites legal**

Denmark (where I happen to live) has some of the toughest consumer-protection laws in the world and these have been recently rewritten to incorporate e-commerce. As a result, potential e-customers are now entitled to much more information regarding product functionality and maintenance, shelf life, health warnings, etc. There are new regulations as to how consumers can pay for their purchases electronically, and to what extent a site owner can ask for personal information that is not directly relevant to the purchasing process (the sex of the purchaser, for example, is generally irrelevant and cannot therefore constitute required data). There are even strict guidelines as to how and where an address and phone number are located on the site. Finally, all Danish e-commerce sites must now provide the same 14-day money-back guarantees that are required of brick-and-mortar operations.

Not surprisingly, on 1 July 2000, when the new (and badly publicized) laws went into effect, the vast majority of Danish e-commerce site owners suddenly found themselves operating illegally. Information architects must therefore be aware of two things.

First, if you're working on a full-blown e-commerce site, you must talk to the site owner's legal advisors to determine the type of detailed content needed to meet current national legislation. Invariably this information serves to improve the shared reference (see Chapter 6). Second, if personalization and customization features rely on user-supplied information and/or cookies, make sure this information is acquired and used in a legally acceptable manner.

Granted, the Danes are rather gung-ho when it comes to consumer protection, but my legal contacts elsewhere in the world tell me that similar laws are in the works throughout much of the European Union as well as in North America. In short, *caveat lector*!

One interesting factor that may come out of all this is that national URLs may enjoy increased popularity over the more general ".com" suffixes if these suggest a greater measure of consumer protection. That said, since a URL can reside almost on any server, anywhere in the world, this may never come about, but it's certainly food for thought.

19.11 Increased emphasis on personalization

If one of our goals, as information architects, is to reduce the visibility of the hierarchy and to surface relevant information, the ultimate solution would seem to be to do away with the traditional, fixed hierarchy entirely.

For example, I'd love to land on a homepage, type or speak a plain-language request, and have the site generate a structure "on the fly" designed to meet my unique needs – a "dynamic hierarchy" if you will. Although current collaborative filtering technology can, to some extent, anticipate my perceived needs, this is really just a sophisticated form of second-guessing that serves to improve contextual navigation but rarely eliminates distracting junk.

For any of this to happen, though, we must accept the fact that computers are no more mind-readers than people are. Thus, there is a major need to find better and less intimidating ways to get people to *tell* us what they want. Already, AltaVista lets users type in plain-language queries based on technology developed by "Ask Jeeves." Without knowing the specifics involved, in many ways, the inner workings of the AltaVista interface seem remarkably similar to the artificial intelligence parsers I worked with when writing computer adventure games back in the early 1980s. These parsers helped interpret complex requests such as "take the golden sword and kill the drooling giant." Given our need for better two-way communication, I think artificial intelligence has a large role to play in the coming years in the interpretation of a visitor's declared mission. And, quite frankly, even if a computerized voice one day tells me, "Sorry.

I can't help you," I think I'd be grateful the site was honest and didn't waste my time.

19.12 A final thought

We're all pioneers in an untamed electronic world and most of the "rights" and "wrongs" of information architecture have yet to be defined. Until they are, we must content ourselves with "better" and "worse." In the meantime:

- Remain open
- Be flexible
- Use your common sense
- Listen

Appendix A

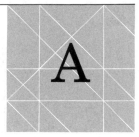

Sample editorial content sheet

Page number:

Page title:

Target audience:

Basic description:

Suggested graphic elements:

Other special features:

Special informational needs:

Suggested hyperlinks from main content area:

Information source(s):

Editorial content to be provided in following file format:

Content provider(s):

Deadline:

Content to be approved by:

Sample editorial content sheet (filled in)

Page number: 2.1.1

Page title: XJ-140 Super Widget

Target audience: Construction engineers

Basic description: Main product presentation page for XJ-140

Suggested graphic elements: Photo of XJ-140, cut-away diagram showing special reverse-flow detector.

Other special features: It would be nice to have an animation of the reverse-flow detector.

Special informational needs: We need to define our RFD technology (reverse-flow detection). The XJ-140 base mount has just been redesigned for easier installation.

Suggested hyperlinks from main content area: 2.1.1.1 Technical data, 2.1.1.2 Safety specifications, 5.2.1 Customer reference, 2.1.4.3 Accessories

Information source(s): Printed product catalog, page 83. Also, talk to Mary in R&D, extension 433. CAD drawings can be obtained from Frank, extension 237.

Editorial content to be provided in following file format: MS Word 6.0

Content provider(s): Rick (text), Jan (graphics)

Deadline: March 23

Content to be approved by: Jack

Glossary

For your convenience, here's an alphabetical list of my definitions of some current web terminology. Apart from its revised structure and some contextual editing, it is essentially the same as that found in Chapter 1.

For those of you who are wondering why this list appears twice, let me explain: I put this information in the first chapter as a list of related words so that new readers could quickly gain an overview of what I meant when I used a particular term. Since related words don't necessarily come next to each other in an alphabetical list, I chose to arrange them differently. The alphabetical structure provided here helps you find something when you *know* what you're looking for.

architecture often this term is synonymous with structure, although structure usually refers to a specific project-related diagram whereas architecture relates more to the overall generic concept of informational organization.

content this word has two distinct uses in this book. In most instances, content refers merely to the *subject* discussed on a particular page. However, in rare instances it may indicate editorial content, which refers to specific information.

content management the process of transferring editorial content (text and graphics) to a website in a controlled and organized manner and/or editing existing browser-based content.

content provider someone who supplies editorial content, usually written, although photographs and graphics are also editorial-content elements.

contextual navigation the collection of related links on a page that allows visitors to immediately click to subject-related pages, even when these pages actually live under another menu heading. In traditional library terms, this is known as "cross-referencing."

customization what a visitor does to a site when setting personal preferences (turning off graphics, arranging content, etc.). Not to be confused with *personalization*, which is what a site does to itself in anticipation of a visitor's needs.

design within the context of this book, design almost always refers to the visual appearance of a web page. Design elements include all graphics, such as buttons, logos, animations, photographs, etc., plus background colors and text fonts. That said, I sometimes use the phrase "designing a site" in the broader sense to reflect both structural *and* graphical considerations.

drop-down a menu that expands when it is clicked, for example, those menus located at the top of the screen in virtually all Windows and Macintosh applications.

e-business a broad, catch-all term for the transactions and other business operations that use the web as the basic communications infrastructure. In other words, a company can practice e-business by using their site for lead generation without actually conducting e-commerce.

e-commerce the specific process of selling goods or services from a website.

editorial content refers to *specific information*, including all the words, photographs, graphics, and other page-specific elements that appear on a site. Sometimes I've shortened editorial content to content for the sake of readability if the proper context seemed obvious.

granularity the extent to which a larger piece of information has been broken down into smaller units. For example, this book is broken down into individual chapters, each of which features its own set of sections. The content of an individual subhead is the smallest "grain" in this particular work although the index helps identify even smaller grains. On a website, the more subdivisions you create in a document, the greater the granularity and thus the greater the dynamics of the site. There are limitations, though – after all, sometimes a cracker is better than a handful of crumbs.

GUI (Graphical User Interface) the revolutionary "desktop-cursor-icon" concept (including menus, folders, and files) developed by Xerox PARC in the 1970s, first exploited commercially by Apple in 1983 with the launch of the Macintosh. Xerox PARC's use of the computer mouse for point-and-click operations was also an integral part of this concept.

HCI (Human–Computer Interaction) the study of how people relate to electronic tools and interfaces. Also called CHI.

homepage generally, the first page that greets a visitor when visiting a particular website. Some people still insist on referring to the entire site as a homepage, which is a hangover from the old days when a site rarely *had* more than one page. If you're still calling websites homepages, it's time you got out of the habit!

HTML (HyperText Markup Language) the programming language used to create websites, the brainchild of WWW founder Tim Berners-Lee.

hyperlink for the purposes of this book, a hyperlink is a link that forms part of the editorial content of the page rather than a graphic button in the primary navigation. In most instances, hyperlinks are set in the ordinary text font, underlined, and given a contrasting color. However, small graphics can also function as hyperlinks if they are located within the content area of the page.

layout the physical positioning of graphic and text elements on a web page.

link any text or graphic device that brings visitors to a new page when clicked.

local navigation navigational choices leading to subtopics defined by one of the main-menu subjects.

main menu often used as a synonym for homepage, but in the strictest terms refers specifically to the top-level navigational choices. I use the phrase in both ways.

menu a list of choices. In web terms, these choices usually function as individual links to other pages.

page all the information that appears on the screen following a single mouse-click.

personalization what a site *does to itself* in terms of altering navigation according to the perceived needs of an individual visitor. By and large, personalization is used to provide improved contextual navigation.

pop-up a small screen or graphic "bubble" that is superimposed on a screen when you click a particular area. For example, many Windows programs use pop-up "help" bubbles.

primary navigation the general menu choices that are repeated on most (if not all) of the pages contained in the site. Sometimes called the main menu.

rollover a dynamic device that changes the appearance of the page when the cursor moves over a particular area without the user having to click. Buttons that change color when the cursor is correctly positioned are rollovers. However, sometimes rollovers can contain explanatory text, particularly in conjunction with a diagram or photograph.

site synonymous with website

site owner the person or organization with overall responsibility for the design and editorial content of the site. For example, AltaVista would be the site owner for the search engine Altavista.com.

site tools sometimes called global navigation or functional navigation, devices in this category refer to search engines, site maps, etc. that let you immediately jump from one page on the site to another without drilling down through a hierarchy. Site tools, however, can also include the contact page and other subjects of a more general, practical nature.

splash screen one or more pages that have been designed to welcome a visitor to the main page of a website. A large corporate logo with a hyperlink stating "Click here to enter site" is a typical example. Also called an "entry tunnel." Navigational options are usually quite limited, but sometimes these screens are used by international organizations to give visitors a choice of languages before they enter the site proper.

structure the detailed diagram or text outline that indicates the subject content of every page in a website and how it relates to the other pages on the site or links to external pages. Many professional information architects call these "Visiograms," named after the PC program used to create them.

subpage a page (generally more detailed) related directly to some preceding page.

subsite an autonomous site, often with a narrow target audience, that is a spin-off from another site, generally with a broader audience. Sometimes for purposes of differentiation, the more general site is called the main site, although occasionally, two related sites may regard each other as subsites. CNN.com and the subsite for Sports Illustrated magazine, CNNSI.com, are a good case in point.

surface often used as a verb as in "to surface information," which means to bring information to a higher level within the overall hierarchy or to create contextual links that make it easier for visitors to find related information located elsewhere on the site.

syndicated content dynamic editorial content created by a third party and made available for wider distribution via subscription. For example, stock prices on a banking site are a classic example of syndicated content.

taxonomy the study of the general principles of scientific classification. Often, information architects use the term to represent a particular hierarchical structure. For example, the underlying structures of two distinct main-menu choices may be referred to as "parallel taxonomies."

UML (Unified Modeling Language) an object-oriented analysis/design method for visualizing, specifying, constructing, and documenting informational relationships – a hot information architecture topic these days.

URL (Uniform Resource Locator) the means by which an exact location on the internet is identified – an innovation of Tim Berners-Lee, the founder of the world wide web. The URL appears in the address line in the browser window, for example, http://www.anywhere.com.

usability for the purposes of this book, usability deals with how visitors perceive the *functionality* of a particular website. The ergonomic aspects of usability (for example, whether visitors can actually *find* a particular link on a screen) are not discussed in any detail. In fact, I've tried to avoid graphic-design issues as much as possible. Please check the reading list at the back of this book for additional references.

visitor a person who enters a website. Sometimes called a user, although I generally prefer visitor since this implies that the person in question is an outsider rather than someone directly connected with the site owner's organization. On the other hand, since a website is really an *application*, visitors are, in fact, users and I therefore use both terms.

WAP (Wireless Application Protocol) an open communication standard that allows people to access dynamic content from mobile devices, primarily telephones.

web refers to the World Wide Web (WWW), which, for our purposes here, is more or less synonymous with the internet, although technically speaking the internet is a physical structure and the web is what the internet became with the introduction of HTML.

website represents the complete interrelated collection of pages and links that are created and maintained by a single owner.

wireframes the skeletal design templates for generic pages, indicating the correct position of individual elements including text, graphics, navigation, banner ads, etc.

Further reading

If you want to learn more about some of the subjects I've touched on, these books are good places to start. This is by no means a comprehensive list, nor is it even an "essential library." It's merely a list of references that I've personally found useful among the thousands of books currently available, although I don't always agree with the conclusions of these authors.

Information architecture

Rosenfeld, Lou and Peter Morville. *Information Architecture for the World Wide Web*. Sebastopol, CA: O'Reilly, 1998.

Usability

Cooper, Alan. *The Inmates Are Running the Asylum: Why High-Tech Products Drive Us Crazy and How to Restore the Sanity*. Indianapolis, IN: Sams, 1999.

Nielsen, Jakob. *Designing Web Usability*. Indianapolis, IN: New Riders, 2000.

Norman, Donald A. *The Design of Everyday Things*. New York, NY: Doubleday/Currency, 1989.

Rubin, Jeffry. *Handbook of Usability Testing: How to Plan, Design, and Conduct Effective Tests*. New York, NY: John Wiley & Sons, 1994.

Tenner, Edward. *Why Things Bite Back: Technology and the Revenge of Unintended Consequences*. New York, NY: Vintage, 1997.

Navigation and interface design

Fleming, Jennifer. *Web Navigation: Designing the User Experience*. Sebastapol, CA: O'Reilly, 1998.

Head, Alison J. *Design Wise: A Guide for Evaluating the Interface Design of Information Resources*. Medford, NJ: Information Today, Inc./ CyberAge Books, 1999.

Website design

Andres, Clay. *Great Web Architecture: Top Web Architects Reveal Proven Techniques for Smart and Effective Sites*. Foster City, CA: IDG Books Worldwide, 1999.

Flanders, Vincent and Michael Willis. *Web Pages That Suck: Learn Good Design by Looking at Bad Design*. San Francisco, CA: Sybex, 1998.

Lynch, Patrick J. and Horton, Sarah. *Web Style Guide: Basic Design Principles for Creating Web Sites*. New Haven, CT: Yale University Press, 1999.

Project management

Burdman, Jessica. *Collaborative Web Development: Strategies and Best Practices for Web Teams*. Reading, MA: Addison-Wesley, 1999.

Siegel, David. *Secrets of Successful Websites: Project Management on the World Wide Web*. New York, NY: Macmillan, 1997.

Organizational research

Beyer, Hugh and Holtzblatt, Karen. *Contextual Design: A Customer-Centered Approach to Systems Design*. San Francisco, CA: Academic Press/Morgan Kaufmann, 1997.

Information management

Brown, John Seeley and Duguid, Paul. *The Social Life of Information*. Boston, MA: Harvard Business School Press, 2000.

Korfhage, Robert R. *Information Storage and Retrieval*. New York, NY: John Wiley & Sons, 1997.

Wurman, Richard S. *Information Anxiety*. New York, NY: Doubleday, 1989.

Business and e-commerce

Dalgleish, Jodie. *Customer-Effective Web Sites: 17 Rules Every E-commerce Site Must Follow*. Upper Saddle River, NJ: FT.com/ Prentice-Hall PTR, 2000.

Forrest, Edward and Richard Mizerski (editors). *Interactive Marketing*. Lincolnwood, IL: NTC Business Books, 1996.

Peppers, Don and Martha Rogers, with Robert Dorf. *The One-to-One Fieldbook: The Complete Toolkit for Implementing a 1-to-1 Marketing Program*. New York, NY: Currency/Doubleday, 1999.

Rosenoer, Jonathan, Douglas Armstrong, and J. Russell Gates. *The Clickable Corporation: Successful Strategies for Capturing the Internet Advantage*. New York, NY: The Free Press, 1999.

Seybold, Patricia B., with Ronni T. Marshak. *Customers.com: How to Create a Profitable Business Strategy for the Internet and Beyond*. New York, NY: Random House, 1998.

Schwartz, Evan I. *Digital Darwinism: Seven Breakthrough Business Strategies for Surviving in the Cutthroat Web Economy*. New York, NY: Broadway Books, 1999.

Schwartz, Evan I. *Webonomics: Nine Essential Principles for Growing Your Business on the World Wide Web*. New York, NY: Broadway Books, 1997.

Web communities

Kim, Amy Jo. *Community Building on the Web: Secret Strategies for Successful Online Communities*. Berkeley, CA: Peachpit Press, 2000.

Index